Mind the Tech Gap

IT and cybersecurity teams have had a long-standing battle between functionality and security. But why? To understand where the problem lies, this book will explore the different job functions, goals, relationships, and other factors that may impact how IT and cybersecurity teams interact. With different levels of budget, competing goals, and a history of lack of communication, there is a lot of work to do to bring these teams together. Empathy and emotional intelligence are common phenomena discussed in leadership books, so why not at the practitioner level? Technical teams are constantly juggling projects, engineering tasks, risk management activities, security configurations, remediating audit findings, and the list goes on. Understanding how psychology and human factors engineering practices can improve both IT and cybersecurity teams can positively impact those relationships, as well as strengthen both functionality and security. There is no reason to have these teams at odds or competing for their own team's mission; align the missions, align the teams. The goal is to identify the problems in your own team or organization and apply the principles within to improve how teams communicate, collaborate, and compromise. Each organization will have its own unique challenges but following the question guide will help to identify other technical gaps horizontally or vertically.

Mind the Tech Gap

Addressing the Conflicts between IT and Security Teams

Dr. Nikki Robinson

CRC Press
Taylor & Francis Group
Boca Raton London New York

CRC Press is an imprint of the
Taylor & Francis Group, an **informa** business

First edition published 2023
by CRC Press
6000 Broken Sound Parkway NW, Suite 300, Boca Raton, FL 33487-2742

and by CRC Press
4 Park Square, Milton Park, Abingdon, Oxon, OX14 4RN

CRC Press is an imprint of Taylor & Francis Group, LLC

Library of Congress Cataloging-in-Publication Data
Names: Robinson, Nikki, author.
Title: Mind the tech gap : addressing the conflicts between IT and security
teams / Nikki Robinson.
Other titles: Mind the technology gap
Description: First edition. | Boca Raton, FL : CRC Press, 2023. |
Series: Security, audit and leadership series | Includes bibliographical
references and index.
Identifiers: LCCN 2022013268 (print) | LCCN 2022013269 (ebook) |
ISBN 9781032206165 (hbk) | ISBN 9781032206172 (pbk) | ISBN 9781003264422 (ebk)
Subjects: LCSH: Communication of technical information. | Information
technology—Management. | Computer networks—Security measures. |
Communication in organizations.
Classification: LCC T10.5 .R54 2023 (print) | LCC T10.5 (ebook) |
DDC 601/.4—dc23/eng/20220722
LC record available at https://lccn.loc.gov/2022013268
LC ebook record available at https://lccn.loc.gov/2022013269

ISBN: 9781032206165 (hbk)
ISBN: 9781032206172 (pbk)
ISBN: 9781003264422 (ebk)

DOI: 10.1201/9781003264422

Typeset in Sabon
by codeMantra

Dedication

I dedicate this book to my husband and daughters. Without their support, love, and encouragement, I wouldn't have been able to do this. To Brian – thank you for literally, everything. To my girls – Keira and Teagan – I love you so much. Anything is possible when you work hard and love what you do.

Contents

List of figures

About the author

Nikki Robinson earned a DSc in Cybersecurity and several industry certifications including the Certified Information Systems Security Professional (CISSP), and is a Security Architect by day and an adjunct professor at night. She had more than 10 years of experience in IT operations before moving into the security field about 3 years ago. She studied vulnerability chaining concepts and completed her PhD in Human Factors to combine psychological and technical aspects to improve security programs. She has a passion for teaching and mentoring others on risk management, network defense strategies, and Digital Forensics and Incident Response (DFIR). She is currently a Security Architect and has technical experience in continuous monitoring, risk management, digital forensics, and incident response. She has spoken at several conferences on a variety of topics from human factors security engineering, malicious website graphing, and DevSecOps.

Chapter 1

Background of IT and cybersecurity fields

BACKGROUND

Information Technology (IT) and cybersecurity are both booming fields across a variety of industries and sectors. The explosion of technology in the last 30 years or so has truly expanded the job market. This rapid expansion leads to increased innovation, emerging software, and new types of platforms, as well as an increased technology presence required in all sectors of our world. From the healthcare sector to Industrial Control Systems and Critical Infrastructure, the way business is conducted is changing. Organizations that expand rapidly, develop software quickly and efficiently, are hailed as innovative and leaders in their respective fields.

This seemingly infinite expansion of technology has improved speed of manufacturing, ability to quickly iterate in application development, as well as ability to start and develop a business. Building a company from the ground up is so much easier with website templates available, cloud infrastructure available within seconds, and ability to communicate quickly with potential partners or distributors. However, with increased availability, visibility, and interconnected organizations, what risks, or security issues, can occur with the rise of ever-evolving technology? Given the increased telework and mobile requirements of organizations, IT, development, and cybersecurity teams are constantly under pressure to learn and grow with emerging technology.

When IT became defined as its own field in the 1970s, there were many positions available for individuals interested in this profession. Helpdesk, systems administration, systems engineering, software engineering, network engineering, and infrastructure architects were all available as possible roles. As these roles were just a few of the basics, it was also possible to expand into a specific field or technology, for example, an individual could become a Microsoft Active Directory specialist as their full-time role in more recent times. This is still true today, and specialists are highly regarded and needed in specialized or siloed environments.

DOI: 10.1201/9781003264422-1

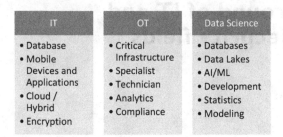

IT	OT	Data Science
• Database • Mobile Devices and Applications • Cloud / Hybrid • Encryption	• Critical Infrastructure • Specialist • Technician • Analytics • Compliance	• Databases • Data Lakes • AI/ML • Development • Statistics • Modeling

Figure 1.1 IT fields and specialties of technology.

HISTORY OF IT

Since the IT field has been around quite a few decades longer than cyber-security, there are longer established principles, more research, and more available resources. The IT field is not only on-premises data centers and mainframes, but it has also now expanded to encompass Internet of Things, Operations Technology, and leveraging Artificial Intelligence and Machine Learning (ML). These may have been buzz words, but these technologies are here to stay and are being integrated constantly into software and applications. Technologists must now expand their own view, field of study, and expertise to keep up with these evolving fields (Figure 1.1).

But individuals within the IT field needed to understand security controls and baselines as a part of their daily tasks, along with other operational and technical requirements. While security professionals did exist around 20 years ago, the field was quite different and focused more on assessments and *technical* controls. Security professionals primarily existed as a last line of defense or would come into projects at the end to provide final guidance or a list of risks associated with the project. There was also a much larger field for physi-cal security, to aid in the configuration and architecture of on-premises data centers.

Technologists are obligated to grow skills and adapt from workstations and laptops to virtual desktops and infrastructure, up to platform services and cloud providers. Technology has evolved from sending an email to an inbox for one user, to creating groups and channels in a communication application tool. Users can now communicate at the speed of thought, and IT and cybersecurity professionals must be just as quick to remediate issues and security findings. Developers must respond to bug findings and resolve issues and security gaps efficiently to meet customer and business needs. Data scientists review larger data sets and solve more complex problems than have existed previously. Organization technology stacks are only increasing in complexity, not becoming more simplistic.

HISTORY OF CYBERSECURITY

Since early in the 2000s, several documents have been provided by the National Institute of Standards and Technology, or NIST, in relation to security frameworks and controls. From patch management to secure configuration, to Internet of Things and Unmanned Aerial Systems security, NIST has provided a wide range of IT and cybersecurity guidance. NIST has provided both technical instruction and frameworks for industry to follow and improve architecture and design of systems. Some organizations may have already adopted NIST frameworks, like the Risk Management Framework and Cybersecurity Framework, private sectors are starting to follow and use these as a backbone for security assessments and policy.

These documents provide a foundation for knowledge on the *process* required for organizations to create a secure environment. These processes may be broad in nature, or more specific as in the case of SP 800-53 series. Utilizing these frameworks is a backbone for many cybersecurity professionals and executive management to follow and build upon for organization-specific policy. The cybersecurity profession has evolved so much over the last 5–10 years but was originally based on Information Assurance (IA) and identifying gaps in security through penetration tests and security assessments. Security has become such a massive field, however, including threat intelligence, digital forensics, mobile device management, Identity and Access Management, risk management, and governance (to name a few) (Figure 1.2).

Given the Executive Order (EO) on Improving Nation's Cybersecurity from the Biden Administration, many industries and organizations are growing their cybersecurity teams immensely. One of the first sections, Section 2, is focused on removing the barriers of information sharing between organizations. But this concept speaks to the other barriers we

Document Title/Area	Date released
Prioritizing Cybersecurity Risk for Enterprise Risk Management	2022
Recommended Criteria for Cybersecurity Labeling for Consumer Internet of Things (IoT)	2022
Software Supply Chain Security Guidance Under EO 14028	2022
Secure Software Development Framework	2022
Blockchain for Access Control Systems	2021
Developing Cyber-Resilient Systems: A Systems Security Engineering Approach	2021

Figure 1.2 NIST documents and release year.

Figure 1.3 White House guidance in diagram format.

have inadvertently set up between teams and organizations that may benefit from collaboration. This section is relevant and important for all organizations to heed as a potential gap for cybersecurity teams.

Based on the EO, what might have been a one- or two-person cybersecurity engineering group may be now budgeted for 10 or even 20 cybersecurity engineers and analysts. Organizations are starting to include cybersecurity at the beginning of projects, including the concept of 'Shift Left' taken from software development teams. Section 3 of this EO mentions the use of adopting Zero Trust Architecture, using cloud platforms, and streamlining data analytics to improve and modernize cybersecurity efforts. Each of these sections speaks to the need to modernize and improve cybersecurity across all sectors. This is important to this reading because of the most recent push to incorporate and elevate cybersecurity programs, where there may have been a lack of focus or budget previously (Figure 1.3).

WHERE IT MEETS CYBERSECURITY

An example of how security was originally used in IT teams, a network engineer would be required to understand and implement security guidance. While many network device companies provide best practice guides, many engineers had to learn what would work and what would not by trial and error. There were also controls that could not be implemented because of potential functionality issues, and even though a mitigating control may have been available, they may not have been configured. Another possibility was that a network engineer may have created mitigating controls, but they were not recognized by the security team because they did not fix the specific control. This is where the interest for this book was created – the idea of how two teams may, or may not, work together to come up with a secure and functional solution.

Another example of how IT and cybersecurity roles were previously more linked was a helpdesk technician or systems administrator. Both roles were responsible for working with customers to resolve technical or functionality issues, as well as resolving vulnerabilities on systems. It is also possible that 20 or so years ago, someone on helpdesk may respond to a possible security incident as a first line of defense. The individual may be monitoring emails or reviewing the antivirus management console and determine that malware or a trojan was downloaded. They may respond to the incident, remove the file/s, and run follow-up antivirus scans, or even re-image the machine depending on the level of compromise.

Up to this point, *process* and *technology* have been the primary components of what built up the IT and cybersecurity fields. But that has not been an incredibly successful technique, given that there is a major gap in supporting the *people* that must follow the policies set out by the organization, and use the technology given to them. Without supporting the humans that use and develop the technology required by a modern organization, projects fail, security practices are immature, and organizations have a much harder time maturing in both IT and cybersecurity programs. The people that make up the organization, especially the technical teams that interact, must be supported, and considered as part of the technical and process components (Figure 1.4).

Since the roles could not continue in parallel, they had to become independent fields to allow for separation of duties. Separation of duties ensures that the same person finding the security settings is not enabled and is not the same person that is applying those security controls. With the identification that having IT and cybersecurity roles within the same position could lead to insecure configuration, the tasking and duties evolved into new jobs and job descriptions. A systems administrator who may have been responsible for inventory, patch management, asset configuration, and delivery sheds most of those responsibilities and may be more focused on cloud deployments or a specific technology.

CYBERSECURITY EDUCATION

Cybersecurity is now a major field of interest for universities, including undergraduate to doctorate programs. Cybersecurity education is not limited

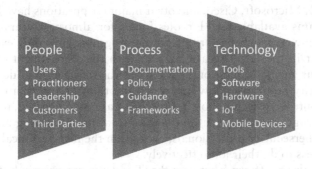

Figure 1.4 People process tech.

to universities, but many training providers have popped up to address technical and specialized fields like Digital Forensics and Incident Response. But this has not always been the case, and cybersecurity was previously known as security or IA. And cybersecurity is the current iteration of this terminology, but it has seen many forms previously. IA was originally meant to improve qualify or quantify risks to information systems, whereas cybersecurity today encompasses a wide variety of skillsets.

There has also been a major increase of use for cybersecurity and IT hands-on labs. Individuals within cybersecurity need to understand the technical implications of security controls across multiple types of technology. This requirement for the use of multiple types of technology is also instrumental in a successful IT career. Multiple training organizations now require a hands-on learning component to demonstrate technical ability to resolve problems. This ensures in-depth understanding for either a specific technology or type of security domain. For example, the Offensive Security Certified Professional by Offensive-Security requires a 24-hour hands-on lab to complete the certification requirement, as well as a written report.

Education and available training have widely varied for IT and cybersecurity professionals. Twenty years ago, computer programming and computer science were common undergraduate degrees available for anyone interested in an IT career. For cybersecurity professionals, IA degrees may have been available but were more likely a concentration for an IT or computer science degree. Training for cybersecurity began with the CompTIA Security+ certification that grew in popularity due to the Department of Defense 8570 requirement for contractors issued in 2005. From this initial security certification, many organizations and available certifications exist today, from the Certified Incident Handler by SANS to Certified Threat Intelligence Analysts by EC-Council.

IT EDUCATION

IT training has been available from major companies such as Microsoft since 1992. Microsoft, Cisco, and other major corporations have had training programs available for IT professionals for almost 30 years as of this writing. However, cybersecurity training programs have only exploded in the market in the last 10 years, as seen with the Department of Defense 8570 requirement. A question arises about the maturity and depth of the cybersecurity programs. How can we ensure that the speed of technology and the controls to secure those technologies are encompassed, in depth, in training programs? This question alludes to a major training and skillset gap for cybersecurity professionals; even given the high technical skill they must possess to do their jobs effectively.

There is also a difference between the IT and cybersecurity industries when it comes to what certifications are most beneficial, and even if certifications should be required. There has been an interesting debate within both communities on which certifications are required. IT or cybersecurity contracts may require a certain number of certifications or based in a specific technology. However, IT and cybersecurity professionals may disagree on the value or utilization of certifications within their organizations. Where an IT professional may focus on a specific technology, like the 'Microsoft Certified' series, cybersecurity certifications may be broader or vendor-agnostic like the ICS2 Certified Information Systems Security Professional (CISSP) or the CompTIA Security+, as previously mentioned.

Cybersecurity-specific programs may come from more vendor-agnostic vendors like SANS or EC-Council. One of the major benefits here is that the concepts may be applied across a variety of software and technologies. The cybersecurity domain of incident response could be studied in a broad way but be utilized in small- to medium-sized businesses or local institutions. While there may be nuance to customers, strategic vision or types of technologies used, the principles of Incident Response remain the same. A security analyst may respond differently to malware on one workstation vs a Denial of Service attack, but the communication methods for an incident would be defined regardless of the type of organization.

The IT certification paths have grown exponentially; just searching the Microsoft Certified catalog, one can find over 250 available certifications. Other major tech companies such as Cisco, Citrix, McAfee, and Linux have their own certifications or institutes dedicated to providing courses and certification paths. Aside from vendor-centric certifications, organizations including CompTIA, EC-Council, SANS, and ISC2 provide specific certifications in both IT and cybersecurity disciplines. These organizations provide certifications and courses available for entry-level up to expert IT and cybersecurity professionals. There are also training programs available for software developers or data scientists interested in Artificial Intelligence/Machine Learning, like AWS, Oracle, and RedHat.

SOFTWARE DEVELOPERS

As software development and cloud platforms have grown, more systems are either built in cloud platforms or use a mixture of on-premises and cloud. Many organizations are currently moving toward a cloud native environment and moving to micro-services and removing physical infrastructure all together. This evolution has changed the way that IT and cybersecurity groups work together and exist as teams. IT teams do not look the same way they did even 5 years ago, and cybersecurity roles and teams are changing every day. And even as I am writing this book, there is likely a new method of software development or cybersecurity practice that will be missing. But the core problem stays the same – the lack of communication and coordination between IT and cybersecurity teams.

Another example of major job duties and responsibilities shifting in recent history are software developers. Several years ago, developers had slower cycles for development and testing, and typically used a waterfall methodology for development cycles. The waterfall methodology was a linear way of programming, and the code was not necessarily fixed for bugs or security issues until after it was pushed to production. But with the development and adoption of agile methods, code is constantly reviewed, tested, and pushed to production. This limits the time from development to production, as well as shortening the time from finding bugs, to resolving them.

Major organizations have software development cycles which could be done monthly, weekly, or even daily as in the case with Netflix. The Netflix DevOps model, which is the combination of Development and Operations groups and tasking, has become an industry-wide golden standard. Their teams can develop and iterate code daily, which has completely changed the way developers think about and code for customers. This increased speed from development to production also changes the way we consider how security is integrated into that process. Hence, the newer field of DevSecOps, which is the combination of developers, security, and operations teams, has encouraged aligned processes and goals.

MAJOR SHIFTS IN IT/CYBERSECURITY

With the constant changes to both the IT and cybersecurity fields, it is possible that there is upskilling, job rotation, or working to improve collaboration and communication between teams. It may already be difficult for organizations to have a comprehensive and effective communication plan to work between Human Resources and Finance. To this point, there may already be difficult communications between IT and cybersecurity groups simply based on the idea that they have different objectives. IT groups are primarily focused on the business and the functionality for users, whereas cybersecurity groups are concerned with risk and the overall security landscape of the organization.

One such change in cybersecurity has been the constant new fields and domains developed within the industry. The focus of DevSecOps is new within the past few years and requires a specific blend of skills between software engineering and security in-depth understanding. It is the integration of development, operations, and security teams from the onset of projects. This integration of teams early on allows for faster and more agile development, integration of security during weekly or bi-weekly sprints, and increased success rate in projects. Without this early integration, security assessments may be left to the end of development projects, which ultimately leads to either delays to production or releasing insecurity products (Figure 1.5).

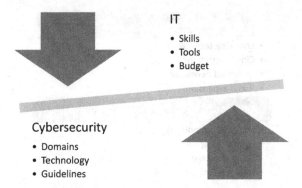

Figure 1.5 Gaps between IT and cybersecurity groups.

WHAT IS THE PROBLEM?

This book aims to identify and understand the technical and security gaps between IT and cybersecurity teams, as well as provide guidance and possible solutions for addressing these issues. Both the IT and cybersecurity professionals have changed tremendously in the last 20 years, and our organizations need to understand that there may be contention or gaps between those teams. And when these gaps or issues occur, it can affect the functionality or security of many types of organizations. Something as simple as an email, phone call, or one meeting can severely impact the length of time from identifying vulnerabilities to remediating. Each interaction between IT and cybersecurity groups can have impact on the security and functionality of the environment.

Without a comprehensive review of the *people* behind the IT and cybersecurity teams, we may not understand the full scope of problems and complexity of miscommunication leading to insecure environments. Having the latest *technology* and most impressive and mature *processes* may not address the root of the problem behind our IT and cybersecurity projects and goals. Even with a holistic security program plan, there may still be vulnerabilities, major risks, and inability to address threats to an organization. Without even knowing it, organizations may be more susceptible to cyberattacks and never reach full maturity of their cybersecurity programs until they investigate and address potential problems between IT and cybersecurity teams.

To understand the scale of the problem, IT and cybersecurity jobs and tasking will be covered to lay the groundwork for how these teams operate and communicate. Typical IT roles include helpdesk technician, systems administrator, systems engineer, and cloud administrators. And on the cybersecurity side, there are several roles to explore like security analysts, security engineers, digital forensics experts, and incident response analysts. Each role will be covered in depth for types of job duties, technologies they may work with, and

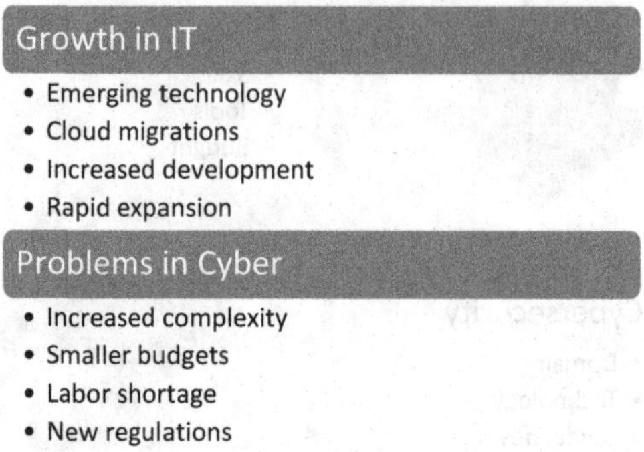

Growth in IT

- Emerging technology
- Cloud migrations
- Increased development
- Rapid expansion

Problems in Cyber

- Increased complexity
- Smaller budgets
- Labor shortage
- New regulations

Figure 1.6 Growth in IT and cyber problems diagram.

teams they interact with. It is important to understand how these roles operate separately, as well as how they interact daily on projects and ongoing tasks.

To tie together these roles, we will investigate how these teams communicate and collaborate, thus providing an overview of where IT meets cybersecurity. For example, a developer may not interact with cybersecurity personnel unless receiving vulnerability reports or stage-gate reviews on security issues. At larger and more mature organizations, security teams may be integrated within development and IT teams, but this has not historically been the case. It is also possible that at larger organizations, there is a siloed structure where there may be many different security teams with varied skillsets and responsibilities. These siloed teams can lead to insecure configuration, complex vulnerability management issues, and technical debt which is difficult to categorize (Figure 1.6).

These IT and cybersecurity concerns grow in complexity as these problems linger without resolution. As an organization develops, additional technology projects, application development, and complications arise in the tech stack. The traditional methods and structure for IT and cybersecurity programs do not support new and emerging technology, constantly changing cybersecurity ecosystems, and the increased speed of development and testing. Consider how the technology landscaped looked even 5 years ago, compared to today. Traditional job titles and descriptions, program structure, and organizational support for these programs must evolve to meet the consistent changes in both IT and cybersecurity domains. Without agility throughout these programs, they will never reach full maturity or be able to retain technical employees.

Chapter 2

Roles and responsibilities in IT

ROLES IN IT

Information Technology (IT) is an essential role within any organization, and administrators manage technical upgrades and infrastructure (whether on-premises, virtual, or in the cloud), handle operations issues, and manage relationships with users and management. IT operations groups may be smaller and need to be agile to handle outages and technical issues for customers. Whether supporting internal IT operations or outside customer applications, they play an essential role in keeping the business running. Without a skilled and efficient operations crew, an IT infrastructure may be unstable or riddled with security vulnerabilities. However, IT teams also need management buy-in and support to continue to support systems and upgrade where necessary to meet functionality or security requirements.

As expressed in Chapter 1, there are several fields within IT. Each discipline has its own unique skillset, job duties, and responsibilities to the business. From helpdesk to systems administration and database administration, IT roles have evolved significantly in the past 20 years. For example, helpdesk used to be a primarily on-site role, available for on-site remediation of issues and setting up conference rooms, equipment, and even cabling. Now, helpdesk can be an outsourced function that is primarily housed in a call center. It may also be an online chat function available for employees to troubleshoot simple or well-known issues.

Given the number of applications, infrastructure, and types of business that require support in an organization, skillsets and job roles are varied within IT. To fully understand the scope of IT responsibilities, and how those roles could lead to potential communication or technical issues, each role will be covered in depth. From technical skills and emotional intelligence to day-to-day operations, as well as a case or scenario, will be discussed to highlight the complexity of interactions and job duties for each role.

Roles covered in this chapter will span from helpdesk, IT operations, and software development, to network and systems engineers. Understanding the nuance between those roles helps to provide insight into where problems arise in interactions. It will also be essential to highlight the shifting roles

DOI: 10.1201/9781003264422-2

from IT generalist to IT specialist and how these differing skillsets play into potential disagreements with other members of IT and cybersecurity teams. To round out the chapter, more specialized roles like database administrators (DBAs), data scientists and cloud administrators will also be covered.

HELPDESK

Helpdesk technicians (or administrators) are the front lines of any organizations. While helpdesk groups in the past were typically on-site, it is more common now for helpdesk groups to be either automated with a chatbot or outsourced to other organizations. Historically, helpdesk technicians would handle general user issues like email problems, potential spam, or malware downloads, as well as Operating System (OS) and application issues. They would either answer phone calls from users or respond to emails and ticket requests, depending on what software was available to ingest user complaints.

While in the past a helpdesk technician needed to have a wide variety of skills and technology experience, it is more common now that helpdesk technicians have a very small group of tasks they can resolve. It is more typical now that a script is available, in the case of outsourced helpdesk groups, and they have limited view into customer data as well as the ability to resolve cases. More customer-facing organizations are providing easier access for the users to resolve their own issues or working to create less of a need for an in-house helpdesk. While outsourced, in the case of historical and current helpdesk deployments, it is still very common that helpdesk technicians would have limited permissions or ability to resolve complex issues.

While limited in access, it is still possible that helpdesk technicians had access to a wide variety of technology and applications. Helpdesk is a great place for individuals to learn several different technical skills, while also learning about customer service, service level agreements, and case resolution. In classic IT operations groups, there is a tiered structure in place to ensure that helpdesk is the 'first line of defense'. Higher tiers work on more complex issues and may be more specialized in one specific technology. For example, a Tier II an engineer may be focused on Microsoft Active Directory (AD) and Exchange, and a Tier III engineer might work more on projects and innovation than solely operations work (Figure 2.1).

More often, Tier I helpdesk technicians can gain information on how to resolve tickets, even from a Tier I or Tier II engineer. This allows for upward momentum for helpdesk into Tier II or even into security analyst positions. It is a well-known phenomenon in the industry for high turnover on helpdesk teams due to the ability to learn quickly and specialize in a specific type of technology. There is also a higher instance of burnout due to the stress and long hours for the position. Technicians may also be required for an on-call rotation or work third shift hours from 8 pm to 5 am, for example.

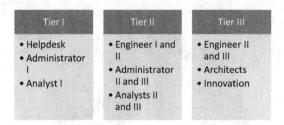

Tier I	Tier II	Tier III
• Helpdesk • Administrator I • Analyst I	• Engineer I and II • Administrator II and III • Analysts II and III	• Engineer II and III • Architects • Innovation

Figure 2.1 Helpdesk tier structure.

While needing to understand a variety of tools and technology, technicians also must have great patience, perseverance, and dedication to resolving issues. The ability to solve problems quickly and efficiently, while potentially learning new applications and technology stacks. For example, a technician may have to solve an email issue, then an antivirus alert, then investigate an account issue, and follow it up with a permissions issue. This requires a level of depth of understanding for how different OS levels interact, how applications function and malfunction, as well as understanding how software functions in a theoretical sense. This theory allows a technician to anticipate where an issue may arise in a specific technology, based on how a tool or application may be built.

While a deep understanding of how technology works is being cemented, technicians are also learning about how to work with and support customers and users. Whether internal or external facing, a helpdesk technicians' best asset is patience and understanding. A mature level of empathy will provide a high success rate for technician and user interactions. It is possible that a user had a horrible drive into work with an hour of unexpected traffic, or maybe they spilled coffee on their lap on the way into work. This user may already be frustrated, and then they attempt to log in to their computer to receive an 'invalid logon attempt' error. Calling helpdesk, maybe even being put on hold, or having difficulty reaching someone, by the time the user reaches a technician they may be incredibly angry.

This anger or frustration is more than likely taken out on the helpdesk technician during a call, if it reaches a person versus a bot. In the case of emotional intelligence, an individual must have patience, understanding, empathy, and the ability to communicate effectively with users to succeed on a helpdesk. Technical skills and control over emotions are almost evenly matched, as answers can be found for users, but working well with them is just as important. If a user does not trust the technician, or does not feel supported, they may complain to management or give a poor customer survey review. This would reflect poorly on the technician and may affect pay raises, upward career movement, or even affect their job stability.

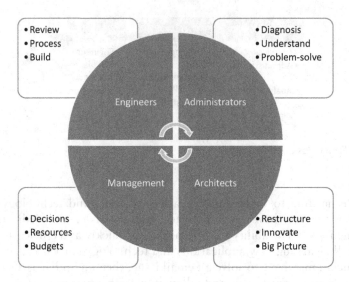

Figure 2.2 Lack of communication diagram.

But working with customers is not the only group of people to interact with, they must also interact with Tier II and Tier III engineers, management, or team leadership, as well as developers and security teams. The ability to communicate technical concerns upwards to potentially more specialized administrators or engineers, as well as to project and product managers is an essential skill. Without this communication, user frustration may rise, as well as the relationships between the technician and engineers. A Tier II or Tier III engineer, if given bad information on a case, may not trust the technician's ability to diagnose or troubleshoot problems for users (Figure 2.2).

This lack of trust due to poor communication could lead to delayed closing of user tickets, longer time to diagnose widespread technical issues, and could even have a trickle effect to how management communicates problems up to higher leadership. Improper diagnosis can lead to conflict between helpdesk and even between the higher tiers of engineers. It could also lead to disagreement between team leadership and management on how cases are handled for customers. This initial assessment of helpdesk technicians highlights how even the frontline defense between users and IT operations groups can lead to discord and confusion on technical issues.

SYSTEMS ENGINEERING

The systems engineering profession encompasses a wide variety of skills and expertise in the entire technology stack. Systems engineers may advance their careers from a helpdesk or systems administrator role. A systems engineer

Figure 2.3 Systems engineering responsibilities and comms matrix.

may be an IT generalist or and IT specialist, which will be discussed later within this chapter. This group of professionals is more widely spread across industries in all sectors. Historically, the term more broadly described a group of technical individuals who may work in the tiered structure mentioned in the previous section (Figure 2.3).

Systems engineers are highly technical and skilled individuals, focused on solving complex problems across the technology stack. Problems may range from a misconfiguration of an application causing user functionality issues, to working with project managers on implementing new software. For example, an engineer may work in the morning on applying patches to their systems, and then in the afternoon meet with a project manager on implementing a new two-factor authentication mechanism. This engineer may specialize in a particular technology, like a Citrix suite of products, or may manage an entire organizations infrastructure from desktop and mobile deployments to managing security monitoring tools.

More recently, systems engineers may step in when helpdesk technicians need assistance, and are focused on more complex issues for the organization. They may be part of a tiered structure for solving user issues, or more internal facing to identify and resolve operations issues. For example, an engineer may develop a test laboratory to create a space to test patches or configuration changes. Another function may be to pilot new systems monitoring software including creating new servers, installing the application, configuring, and then reporting on this to management.

These technical skills are essential to keep any business running, but even more importantly, systems engineers must speak to both technical and non-technical audiences. Without the ability to communicate technical challenges, quite simply, projects fail. If a systems engineer is unable to explain the advantages or disadvantages of a product successfully, management may make the wrong decision and reduce functionality or security of their technology stack. If an encryption software installation affects the virtualization technology in pilot, but it is not communicated as an issue to management, it may be approved and installed in the environment. This issue may grow and affect virtual desktop users, and once the encryption software is installed it could be too difficult to remove from the environment.

This ability to effectively communicate problems to a non-technical audience is essential. Extracting the non-technical details to provide the best decision-making information to leadership is vital to a successful partnership. Engineers must also collaborate with other teams within a large organization. They must also coordinate customer tickets and resolution information with helpdesk or lower tiers in a tiered structure. Working with project management includes providing updates on timelines, delays, and expressing urgency for software or needs for cloud/virtual resources.

Discord arises when systems engineers are not able to properly express their needs, possible issues, or concerns with a particular technology. Mistrust in an engineer occurs very quickly when they try to hide an issue or does not provide all the pertinent information. For example, if an engineer sees a functionality or operational issue but does not disclose this to management, the engineer could ruin a relationship. There is a fine line between fixing small issues before users notice, but if users do notice, and management is not notified, the engineer may face consequences either by reputation or in job status.

NETWORK ENGINEER

Network engineers are a highly technical group of people, primarily focused on networking technologies like routing, switching, and the latest in networking techniques like micro-segmentation (Oggerino, 2017). They are a specialized group of engineers who thoroughly understand and manage a networking infrastructure. While their focus is on routing network traffic, some might consider them the original security engineers. They have a deep understanding how network traffic is routed, which gives them the unique understanding of understanding benign versus anomalous network behavior (Figure 2.4).

With this depth of understanding comes the ability to troubleshoot and understand technical problems that a systems engineer (not familiar with networking), may not. They may be able to spot patterns, detect anomalous or malicious behavior, and determine root causes for other issues in the technical stack. However, network engineers may be siloed within their team and not have as much interaction with other teams. This is not always the case, but it can be difficult if network engineers are not involved in other technical projects or are unaware of the changing IT infrastructure.

Network engineers may need to collaborate with security teams, operations groups, or upper-level management when problems arise. They may also need to be available to make changes as other teams are integrating new software or upgrading their systems. But these changes may be more of an ask, rather than working with the networking team to determine what might be the best avenue for the change. Again, this may not always be the case, it is possible in very mature organizations that the network engineers' interface with other teams.

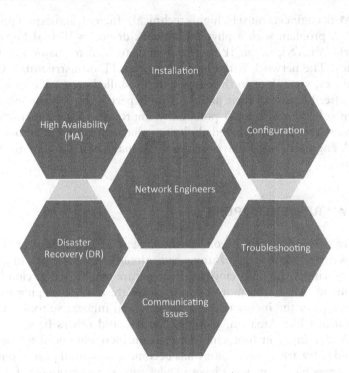

Figure 2.4 Network engineering responsibility matrix.

A network engineer may or may not have a 2- or 4-year degree in IT, tele-communications, or networking. They will more than likely have at least one industry certification in their desired technology. For example, an engineer may pursue certifications for Cisco routing or a Network+ certification from CompTIA. This education provides the technical skills necessary to understand network management and may provide hands-on lab environments. There may be a communication component to this education, but in available online training materials, there does not appear to be a communication or emotional intelligence component to these certifications.

However, in organizations where network teams are siloed, this may lead to difficulty in resolving user functionality issues if they have limited awareness of the organizational structure. It may also be challenging for network engineers to express technical challenges to individuals who are not familiar with networking topologies. Terminology exclusive to managing networks, like spanning tree protocol, mesh topology vs star topology, and trunked ports may not be used in other technical professions. With a basic understanding of network engineers' communication improves, but when an engineer has a deep understanding of these terms and definitions, it can be difficult to explain each term while working through an issue.

Network engineers must be highly technical, efficient, and expert problem-solvers. A problem with a physical network device, a Virtual Local Area Network (VLAN), or an IP-routing issue can lead to major functionality issues. The network is the backbone of an IT infrastructure, whether on-premises, virtual, or in the cloud. Highly skilled network engineers are sought after because of their nuanced and expert abilities. Communication between other groups could potentially improve an operational environment, however. With improved ability to collaborate or work across teams, network engineers would have the insight to make better and more efficient decisions.

SOFTWARE DEVELOPERS

Software developers may be one of the biggest IT professions at the time of this writing. Many organizations have already moved, or are in the process of moving, from on-premises infrastructure to a virtual or cloud-based environment. More and more organizations are also developing in-house software, given the increased need for new and innovative tools. Massive organizations like Amazon, Google, Netflix, and others have a massive software development footprint. There is an incredible need for new and improved software, as technology has become an essential part of our lives.

Developers may or may not have an educational background as far as a 2- or 4-year academic degree. There are several software engineering programs available from small and large institutions, as well as certifications available in programming languages or general software engineering practices. Many certification organizations offer certifications in Java, C or C++, Python, and many other languages. These certifications can be achieved either through the development technology organization, or through a general certification body like ISC2 or CompTIA. These certifications aid software engineers land roles in organizations or can help to display their knowledge in a specific language or framework (Figure 2.5).

This type of role may be the one that has evolved the most over the last 20 years. Developers were typically using a waterfall methodology to manage development cycles, whereas now it is far more accepted to use an agile method. The agile method allows for developers to iterate on a 2-week cycle, versus 6 months to a year to develop and push code to production. The agile process encourages developers to identify and remediate bugs at a much faster pace. There are some organizations, like Netflix, that may even iterate and push code to production daily. This agile methodology encourages developers to resolve issues faster, instead of focusing solely on the end state of a product.

This agile methodology has changed the way developers interact with management and other teams. The term, DevOps, has been coined and used in the last few years to describe the relationship between development and

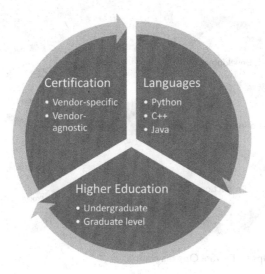

Figure 2.5 Developer certification or education path.

operations groups. Historically, developers worked in a more siloed team to focus strictly on development. They were not responsible for communications, or integrated, with the operations teams that managed the product once it was pushed to production. But in a DevOps and agile workspace, developers work much closer with operations teams to resolve identified issues. And because development cycles are much shorter, security teams are starting to get involved in stage-gate reviews, every 2 weeks, as code is ready to deploy to production.

In the past, security teams may not get involved in development cycles until the code is ready to push to production. This lack of communication and involvement between developers and security teams can lead to many issues. If major security issues were noted after a year of development, the product timeline may get pushed back, increasing cost and resources required. Executive management may get involved once it is noted that a project cannot go to production because of security's findings. This may reflect poorly on the development team, the product team leads, and even the security team for not being involved sooner (Figure 2.6).

With this problem identified across the industry, DevSecOps, or the integration of developers, security teams, and operations groups is changing development cycles again (Myrbakken and Colomo-Palacios, 2017). Security engineers may be involved during the onset of a development project, which allows security teams insight into the architecture of the product and intended outcomes. Security can provide recommendations from the beginning of a project, allowing for increased visibility into possible security issues. These issues can be

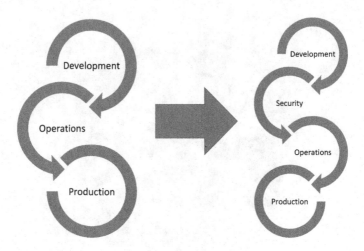

Figure 2.6 DevOps to DevSecOps diagram.

remediated during development cycles and reviewed every 2 weeks during the stage-gate review process.

Developers must now communicate and collaborate with operations teams, security engineers or architects, as well as project and product management. They may also need to connect with users to understand how users will use their products or product testers during development cycles. This ability to empathize and understand requirements, then translate that into code is a most vital skill. It takes the ability to understand user needs and translate human needs into a programming language. This can be a challenging role based on the need to empathize and understand deadlines, project requirements, and keep their technical skills sharp and updated with the evolving development landscape.

DATABASE ADMINISTRATOR/DATA SCIENCE

DBAs and engineers are a very specialized type of technical field where administrators or engineers are primarily focused on the health and management of databases or data lakes. DBA origins lie in the need to understand database administration in depth, whether using a technology like SQL or Oracle. A DBA's primary role is rooted in the ability to architect, implement, and manage database structures. This is an essential role for any organization managing large sets of data, because data integrity could be a major concern in both security and functionality objectives. These administrators and engineers may fulfill operations, engineering, project management, or architecture tasks.

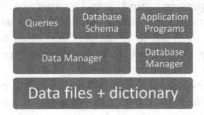

Figure 2.7 **Example of database structure.**

DBAs may hold many responsibilities related to database management, continuous monitoring, Identity and Access Management, as well as data restoration. Large organizations may require complex database structures including clustering and High Availability needs for data. This increases the need for skilled DBAs who can manage these complex environments, massive amounts of data, and ensure data integrity. Depending on the organization, their data may be business proprietary, sensitive, or Personally Identifiable Information which require special storage. DBAs must understand the technical and security requirements for database architecture and design (Figure 2.7).

DBAs more than likely will be involved at the onset of a project, to architect the functional structure for where databases sit in the infrastructure and what technical specifications are needed for type and amount of data. However, if DBAs or engineers are not involved during project inception, they may not fully understand requirements. This could lead to building inefficient databases and clusters, not having the full scope of resources required, or delays from development to production. There could also be disagreement and discord between the DBAs and project management team if deliverables are not met or technical specifications are not laid out from the onset of the project.

Database administration gives way to the field of data science and how data scientists review and parse through large datasets. While not always considered under the IT field umbrella, data scientists working with technologists may influence how we manage and handle large datasets. Data scientists have become a more common field within development, operations, and security teams. They are specialized in identifying and solving problems with large and complex data structures. But they may also be experienced software developers and familiar with many forms of technology, including cloud, databases, networking, and organizational structures.

Data scientists will work with and collaborate with a variety of teams, from customers, IT management, project managers, developers, and operations teams. This collaboration may be required to improve access or integrity to data, as well as understanding current challenges in the tech stack that are contributing to complex organizational issues. This group of individuals, like software developers, must understand a variety of different technologies and be able to understand increasingly complex data structures. They must express these issues in depth to developers and other technical colleagues, while also explaining a path forward to management for budgeting, application development, or resource management.

Without an understanding for user and customer problems versus the types of challenges that developers and operations team experience, a data scientist may have trouble effectively communicating. A user would see a problem differently, and potentially see symptoms dissimilar to what a developer is working on or experiencing. A successful data scientist can collaborate with both types of groups and understand their terminology and own unique challenges. Without this type of collaboration, it could be difficult to understand where the root of the issue is, leading to longer times for troubleshooting or even re-architecting data structures.

CLOUD ADMINISTRATOR/ENGINEER

Cloud technology is on the forefront of where IT infrastructure is headed. More organizations and environments are either moving to a cloud infrastructure or are building cloud native applications. This move comes from the limitations and potential expense that comes from building and maintaining on-premises data centers. Many older organizations are seeing the benefits of migrating to any style of cloud infrastructure, whether fully cloud or in some hybrid capacity. Cloud enables a business to be agile in server and application deployments, as well as potentially improve security, depending on implementation. And given the need for more organizations to increase their digital footprint and provide easier methods for administration, cloud solutions are a major part of the strategy.

Systems administrators have had to upskill or learn more about cloud environments to manage new deployments or migrate current on-premises to a cloud infrastructure. This transition to cloud creates several technical challenges that systems administrators must adapt to and changes troubleshooting efforts and methodologies. Since there are a variety of cloud platforms available, including pay-as-you-go models or stricter environments with data segregation between clients, administrators must learn new technology and methodologies.

Since cloud administrators and engineers are responsible for operations and engineering projects, they may need to learn vendor-specific technology in combination with new terminology and what cloud platforms provide for tools and security. There are three main structures available for cloud environments, Platform as a Service, Software as a Service, and Infrastructure as a Service. Since there are many other 'as a Service' platforms available and are constantly being released, they cannot all be covered in this book. The most

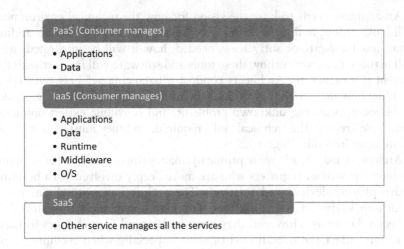

Figure 2.8 Platform as a Service vs Infrastructure as a Service vs Software as a Service.

important note is that cloud administrators and engineers must learn these new terms and skills at lightning pace (Figure 2.8).

Cloud administrators and engineers must learn new tools and technology, build and deploy systems in new environments, and manage business operations. The ability to adapt to new technology and work with multi-disciplined teams is essential to keeping a cloud environment running smoothly. There have been many instances of cloud systems being breached by misconfiguration, which may be due to a lack of understanding or training. These misconfigurations lead to reputation loss for organizations, data loss on massive scales, and even job loss for the cloud administrators. The work in cloud technology is high risk and high reward, adding to the stress and need for precision in configuration and change management.

INFRASTRUCTURE ARCHITECT

Infrastructure architects could go by several titles, including Senior Systems Engineer or Senior Systems Administrator, but here the discussion is focused on how IT professionals improve to look at the technical stack from a 30,000-foot view. Architects at this level are constantly working on integrating new products, rebuilding and improving the infrastructure, as well as aligning the technology with the business objectives and strategy. Individuals who become architects may have been around IT and operations groups for 10–15 years before having enough experience. It is possible someone who moves up to this position is an IT generalist who has worked within a variety of roles in a tech stack, using multiple types of technology.

An architect needs to have the vision for how the technical environment will look, evolve, and grow with the business. This includes understanding what new hardware or software is needed, how it will be integrated, who will manage it, as well as how these tools and software will interact with the current infrastructure. Architects conduct a balancing act between understanding how the current operational environment functions, solving known problems, anticipating unknown problems, and providing expert opinions. And these are only the technical skills required, and they must also communicate at an incredibly high level.

Architects may work with primarily management and executive management, as well as engineers who are more deeply involved with building and deploying devices and software. The architect may not be as much 'hands-on keyboard', meaning that they may not manage these tools on a day-to-day basis. However, they must understand how changes to these tools will affect the overall environment, especially when recommending new tools or removing items from the current infrastructure. Without the depth of knowledge or the ability to communicate with individuals with varying levels of technical experience, an entire organization may be at risk for functionality, budget, or security issues.

An architect may meet challenges if they do not consider all options. For example, if an architect suggests implementing a new third-party application, without consulting the engineers who may end up managing it, there could be serious consequences. First, the engineers may dislike the product and not be able to fully integrate it into their pipelines. Second, the operations crew who is concerned with functionality and was not aware of this new product integration may be frustrated by the lack of communication or involvement during the product selection phase. And finally, with growing frustration between development and operations teams, management may start to distrust architects or implement more thorough reviews for new products.

Based on the possible implications of choosing incorrect or insecure products, architects have a special requirement for communication. Impacts from architect decisions, whether to the operations teams or the customers who consume products, could lead to lost revenue or insecure configurations. The implementation of insecure software or devices, or a breach of exposed systems may even lead to reputation loss within the industry. All good reasons for why an architect must understand the business, work well with other teams, and communicate problems as they arise.

TECHNICAL TEAM LEADS

Technical leads are a special breed of deep technical knowledge, leadership skills, and project management. These leads may manage a small team of technical engineers or administrators, or they may lead product development and design. The experience with hands-on technical roles as a systems administrator or developer facilitates these leads work and collaborate with their technical team members. While not exclusive, having the technical expertise improves the ability for the leads to communicate and collaborate with their team members.

An individual who becomes a technical team lead more than likely started in a highly technical role where they were managing products or services. For example, a Citrix engineer may have moved from managing the Citrix infrastructure, to leading a team of Citrix engineers to maintain the environment. They may hand off daily operations tasks and maintenance to the engineers, while working on upgrade paths and implementation of new applications for users. They may also work more closely with IT management and executive management on goals and objectives for that team.

However, problems may arise in three ways if the technical team lead is not properly suited for the rule. First, if the team lead was promoted but did not want to take on a leadership role, they may not fulfill all of the duties required of a team lead. This could lead to issues between team members and even up through management if they cannot fulfill the management expectations. Second, the team lead may not have enough technical experience to make functionality and operations decisions. The inability to make a proper decision could affect operations, or at the worst, take down the entire infrastructure. And third, the team lead does not work well with other individuals and prefers to work alone as an engineer. If they are forced into this role, they may become disgruntled and ultimately leave the organization.

Technical leadership roles require an individual who is deeply technical but wants to take their role to the next level in a leadership capacity. It is a delicate balance for engineers or developers who may want to grow their role in a more managerial sense. If not done properly, there are major functionality or operations concerns, not to mention possibly not applying security controls. Technical leads are an important component to keep the systems operational, the security posture in check, as well as be the intermediary between management objectives and technical requirements.

OPERATIONAL TECHNOLOGY ENGINEER

Operational Technology (OT) is based on systems that are required to control engines, telecommunications, or industrial processes. Examples of OT systems include any machine that may regulate pressure or temperature, as well as monitor systems to avoid dangerous environments. This term was coined in 2006 (Kamal et al., 2016) and originally applied to power utility control systems but is now applicable to many technologies within Industrial Control Systems. As IT and OT systems have met, with the integration of OT systems control and functionality, IT systems were more aligned with Confidentiality, Integrity, and Availability, or the CIA triad.

OT systems started integrating with IT systems, which led to unique challenges for managing those systems in tandem. OT systems had to meet IT systems where the OT systems had to rely increasingly on IT infrastructure. This connection between OT and IT platforms was dubbed the 'IT OT convergence' (Kamal et al., 2016). Part of the challenges with OT installations and merging with IT infrastructure, is that security is now a much more complex situation. And since OT systems have only recently been recognized as their own set of systems and security requirements, there is little historical context to help manage and secure them.

Along with security challenges, there is an increased need for traditionally OT systems engineers to understand and merge their technology with IT systems. OT engineers must now be able to enhance and upskill to integrate their systems and understand how security impacts this new blended technological infrastructure. OT administrators and engineers are a specialty and separate domain from IT, because of the specialized skills they must possess. In maintaining critical infrastructure systems like electrical or power grids, OT groups must understand highly complex systems.

IT GENERALIST VS IT SPECIALIST

Several of the typical IT fields have been covered, to include helpdesk technicians, systems administrators, and DBAs. But there is a concept within IT of a generalist versus a specialist in the field. An IT generalist may be in a systems administrator or systems engineering role, whereas an IT specialist may have a specific field of engineering, for example a Microsoft Systems Center Configuration Management engineer. These specialties may be in a particular application, OS, or vendor-specific product.

An example of the difference between a generalist would be a cloud engineer versus an Amazon Web Services (AWS) cloud engineer. A cloud engineer may be familiar with and use only AWS but might also be familiar with multiple cloud providers such as Microsoft Azure and Google Cloud Provider. An AWS cloud engineer might have a more in-depth understanding of AWS products and services but could not have as much understanding of the terminology or use of other vendor cloud environments.

A generalist typically understands a variety of products and applications and is not pigeon-holed into one technology. This allows the IT administrator or engineer to grow outside of a specific vendor or application, and potentially move on to be an architect or technical IT manager. A generalist may be more suited for an architect role, given their wide range of experience with infrastructure and how applications work throughout the technology stack. An IT generalist, however, must be able to effectively communicate challenges across the technology stack and understand a variety of products and how they work together or against each other. With a broader view of an entire organizational structure, the generalist may be able to understand business strategy and process from a higher view within the organization.

A specialist may also work as an architect or technical manager but may fit more into a cloud architect or into a specialty area within an organization. The IT specialist will understand deep technical challenges and be able to solve complex issues within their area of expertise. With this deep understanding, the frameworks and troubleshooting methodology may carry from one technology to another. For example, a deep understanding of a Cisco network device does not mean they would not understand another vendor's network device. This allows a deep understanding in their area of expertise and makes specialists excellent problem-solvers.

While an IT generalist may have a broader view of how applications interact and function together, an IT specialist would be more focused on a particular technology or area within the stack. Both types of professionals are needed to truly understand the challenges within an infrastructure and come up with appropriate solutions. But discord may arise when an IT generalist tries to express challenges across the stack, versus a specialist who may be more focused on how it would affect their application or system. This becomes an issue when one feels their problems are of a higher order than the other, or an IT specialist may not be as trusting of an IT generalist's opinion.

A specialist would have a deep understanding of their technical infrastructure and may be concerned if someone who is more of a generalist offers solutions or expresses concerns over changes. This discord could lead to miscommunication of issues, which could impact an entire organization if the lack of communication led to misconfiguration or even accidently taking down a system. For example, an IT generalist recommended a review on a change of a network device because of possible implications to the Virtual Desktop Infrastructure (VDI) environment. The network specialist may push back stating that they do not fully understand the change because they do not understand the technology in depth.

While the above example was focused on network changes, there are possible implications of making changes across the network stack. IT specialists and IT generalists must work together to create a functional and operational environment. They must also have empathy and understanding of how the other operations, a depth versus a broad mindset. Without harmony between the two types of IT professionals, misconfiguration, lack of security controls, and disorganized changed management could occur. A change that goes through a Technical Review Board may take weeks or months, versus a day, if the two groups do not understand and respect the other's concerns and knowledge.

CONCLUSION

As organizations focus increasingly on technology to solve business challenges, IT roles will continue to grow and evolve. From the mostly gone days of using helpdesk as a primary means for root cause analysis and customer support, to moving to on-call or outsourced call centers. Businesses are adapting their business models and IT roles are changing as well. From systems administrators, cloud engineers, and infrastructure architects, to the increasingly complex role of software developers. As business strategy re-aligns with agile, cloud native infrastructure, DevOps, containers, so will roles within the IT field.

Each role in IT may be unique based on the types of technology they manage, user and customer-facing roles, and even what groups they must communicate and coordinate with. Each IT professional has one thing in common however, they must be able to effectively communicate technical and complex problems. They must also translate those complex problems to users, management, customers, or third parties. This skill of communication works well together with the need for understanding how other groups work and their own responsibilities.

Understanding the education, certifications, and classic training associated with IT roles provides an insight into why these roles can be so different. For example, a DBA may not learn how to manage group policies within an AD infrastructure. But it could be beneficial for them to understand what group policy changes mean to their environment and how they may work better with AD administrators. Without a relationship between the groups, it could be difficult to have technical changes made for the database health, coordinate changes that could affect production, or even understand what those changes may mean to the infrastructure.

Specifically in this text, the relationships between IT and cybersecurity groups are of greatest concern. This section built on the knowledge of how different IT roles have evolved, what roles and responsibilities may exist, and what other groups they may need to work with. To understand how IT and cybersecurity groups work together, it is just as essential to understand what roles exist within cybersecurity. Roles within cybersecurity will be explored in relation to responsibilities, skills, technical requirements, and which groups they may need to collaborate with.

REFERENCES

Kamal, S. Z., Al Mubarak, S. M., Scodova, B. D., Naik, P., Flichy, P., & Coffin, G. (2016). IT and OT convergence – Opportunities and challenges. Presented at the SPE *Intelligent Energy International Conference and Exhibition*. Aberdeen, Scotland: UK.

Myrbakken, H., & Colomo-Palacios, R. (2017). DevSecOPs: A multivocal literature review. *International Conference on Software Process Improvement and Capability Determination*. Springer, Cham, 17–29.

Oggerino, C. (2017). Network evolution and network engineering. Retrieved from https://blogs.cisco.com/networking/network-evolution-and-network-engineering.

Chapter 3

Roles and responsibilities in cybersecurity

ROLES IN CYBERSECURITY

The field of cybersecurity has grown immensely in even the last 5 years. With the onslaught of ransomware, Business Email Compromise, Distributed Denial of Service attacks, and many other forms of attack, cybersecurity professionals are highly desired. The field has existed in some form for the last 20 years or so but has evolved at an increasingly rapid pace. Originally, cybersecurity was considered Information Assurance or security, which included physical security as well as security assessments and reports. Network security was also a major field that, while not necessarily called network security at the time, led to new job roles like network security engineers and even security architects.

Organizations are now understanding the impact of not having a robust cybersecurity program. Those implications include losing revenue, reputation, or even having to shut down their entire company due to cybersecurity attacks. Ransomware has made a devastating impact on all manner of organizations, and some companies are never able to financially recover. In brief, ransomware is a form of cyberattack where files are encrypted by a malicious actor and the organization must pay a ransom to receive the decrypt key (Richardson and North, 2017). Without access to files or systems, ransomware may shut down a company for weeks or months, unless a ransom is paid to the individual/s behind the attack. And ransomware is only one form of attack that is easier and easier to conduct, especially with the birth of Ransomware as a Service (RaaS) companies. These companies create and distribute RaaS to malicious actors of all variety to make these types of attacks even simpler to conduct.

Cyberattacks are not only on the rise but are also making a much larger impact in the news media. With a wider lens focused on companies who are impacted by cyberattacks and data breachers, businesses are focusing resources to building more mature cybersecurity programs. This has increased the type and variety of cybersecurity roles available today, and some roles have evolved or encompass more responsibilities. This chapter will cover these roles and how they have changed over time, including security analysts, incident response (IR) teams, red and blue teams, as well as Governance, Risk, and Compliance (GRC).

Each cybersecurity role is unique based on the size and maturity of the cybersecurity program. It is still relatively common to find smaller organizations with no cybersecurity programs, or minimal help available. But this is slowly changing, as more awareness is put on the potential impacts and devastation of cyberattacks, organizations are investing more time and money. To understand these quickly evolving roles, it is important to understand roles and responsibilities, typical technical requirements, associated knowledge of regulations or security control frameworks, as well as what teams they may collaborate with.

It is important to also note, before diving into these roles, that IT and cybersecurity have very different objectives. IT groups are focused on functionality, technology that aligns with the business strategy, as well as operations tasks that could possibly impact users or customers. Cybersecurity professionals are focused primarily on the security and safety of systems and data within the organization. They may still be user or customer facing, but their goal is to protect the businesses' data and critical assets. This difference in objectives is one of the catalysts for miscommunication or misunderstanding between teams.

SECURITY ANALYST

Security analysts are the 'bread and butter' of any security team. They may be part of a Security Operations Center (SOC), or even a Network Operations Center/Security Operations Center. Security analysts operate in a similar fashion to how a helpdesk technical would. IT may manage tickets using ServiceNow or Remedy, where analysts would review alerts from antivirus, antimalware, and Intrusion Detection Systems. They may also both be customer facing, a helpdesk technician may resolve a technical issue for a user, and a security analyst may remove malware or trojans from a workstation. Both work as a sort of 'front lines' technician to resolve smaller issues quickly and efficiently.

A security analyst position is an excellent starting point for a career in cybersecurity, as is helpdesk. Both roles allow an individual to see a wide variety of issues, learn several different tools and technologies, as well as the ability to network with a variety of other teams. A security analyst may work on a malware infection in the morning, check network traffic for anomalies, and monitor vulnerability reports and remediation efforts. They may also be involved in security audits to assist in providing documentation, which provides insight into how audits are conducted and what evidence may be required.

Security analysts in a larger organization may be responsible for a smaller group of tools or security monitoring software, whereas in a smaller business they may be responsible for most or all the security tools. In a smaller team, there may also be a need to handle security assessments, audits, pilot and determine best security tools, as well as work on security projects and recover from incidents. This role is relatively broad and may encompass a wide variety of required skills. With this wide variety of skills and responsibilities can also come a heavy burden which may lead to major burnout of the analyst.

As is the case with helpdesk technicians, analysts must work with users on potential malicious alerts, as well as report to management and even executive leadership in the case of incidents. In a larger organization however, they may be more responsible for continuous monitoring and detection of malicious or anomalous behavior. Continuous monitoring may include monitoring vulnerability scans, reviewing antivirus and antimalware tools and alerts, as well as reviewing secure configuration implementations. Detection of malicious behavior might include reviewing network alerts or looking for suspicious emails and attachments.

But security analysts are also an integral part of cybersecurity teams by communicating with users, management, project leads, HR, executive leadership, IT teams, as well as many others within an organization. They may also work with other cybersecurity professionals like security engineers and architects, as well as digital forensics or insider threat teams when looking for information on an investigation. Depending on the size of the organization, security analysts may have the most responsibility as far as tool configuration and management, as well as handling incidents for customers and users.

SECURITY ASSESSORS/AUDITORS

IT and cybersecurity professionals may be more familiar with the terminology of security assessor/auditor based on the classification structure of cybersecurity professions (NIST, 2011). There are also Security Engineers (SEs) and Security Managers (SMs) that are associated job role categories. Security assessors/auditors are responsible for security assessments, system security plans, testing, and evaluations, among other duties. They may work with SEs for technical evidence or guidance on assessments or policy guidance, and work with SMs on audits, security assessments and reviews, as well as working with systems owners. Security assessors/auditors conduct a variety of job duties but are primarily responsible for the documentation and assessment of systems.

Security assessors/auditors are responsible for understanding and enforcing security control frameworks, like the National Institute of Technology and Standards (NIST) Special Publication (SP) 800-53 rev 5. These documents outline hundreds of security controls, their technical requirements and implementation, as well as justification for application. Along with understanding these controls, security assessors/auditors must understand security frameworks like the NIST Risk Management Framework (RMF) and Cybersecurity Framework. These frameworks outline the full cycle of security assessments, from selection of proper controls and type of systems to implementation, and continuous monitoring.

Integrating frameworks and understanding types of security controls is one essential component of security assessor/auditor responsibilities, as well as understanding different types of systems and what controls or frameworks may be applicable. For example, a standalone system with minimal users may have different controls than public-facing servers with external users and complex infrastructure. Security assessors/auditors must also understand risk management, and how to handle controls that are either not able to be implemented versus controls that may need time or testing before configuring. Exemptions may need to be written up and submitted for approval for controls that are unable to be implemented, whether for functionality issues or technical constraints. Whereas a waiver or risk mitigation strategy may be required for controls that need time for testing, for example a 6-month extension to upgrade OS or applications before the control can be implemented.

Understanding frameworks, controls, waivers, and exemptions, is only the job tasking portion of the responsibilities of security assessors/auditors. They must be able to work with technical Subject Matter Experts (SMEs), system and application owners, systems administrators, network engineers, auditors, and third-party vendors. This ability to communicate effectively across the enterprise is essential to pass audits, properly implement the appropriate security controls, and effectively impact the overall security of the organization. Positive relationships and open lines of communication could mean the success of an audit, or vice versa mean an audit failure which could result in loss of reputation, loss in budget and revenue, and even the inability to use systems until security vulnerabilities are resolved.

If a security assessor/auditor works with a system owner, and requests that they resolve 300 vulnerabilities in 30 days, they may severely impact that relationship. The system owner may feel like they're needs for customers or operations are not being heard or understood and may not respond to emails or instructions from the security assessor/auditor. However, if a security assessor/auditor works with a system owner on a 'get well' plan and steps to get to a more secure state, that would show a collaboration instead of dumping a 300-page vulnerability report and saying, 'fix it'. Similarly, security assessors/auditors must be able to effectively communicate potential issues early, to avoid issues with security audits and assessments.

An auditor coming to an organization for an annual audit will expect certain documentation and evidence available for review. A security assessor/auditor is responsible for coordinating and collecting this information either before the audit, or during, and respond quickly and with the correct information. If a negative experience has given a negative bias from a system owner toward a security assessor/auditor, this information may be difficult to attain and could affect audit results. Whereas a positive relationship could ensure timely information and documentation is available for auditors. Auditors with a positive experience will be able to trust the information given to them, process the audit quickly, and ultimately move on to their next project faster.

SECURITY ENGINEERS (SEs)

A Security Engineer (SE) may also be referred to as an information security engineer, depending on the type of environment. An SE, or security engineer, holds a variety of responsibilities in a security program. A security engineer may either work directly on software development projects and programs or work more as a technical SME across the entire organization. Responsibilities might include network security, continuous monitoring, IR, and automating security tasking, to name a few. In a smaller organization a security engineer may manage and monitor multiple products, like a security analyst, but may also provide development or scripting expertise.

An SE would work with security assessors/auditors to provide technical guidance on implementing controls. They would provide either screenshots or specific instructions for implementing the requested controls or finding mitigating controls to resolve the vulnerability and not affect functionality. They may also get involved if an application or system owner is unsure of how to resolve a vulnerability. An SE is highly technical and able to understand the operations implications of setting certain controls and would be an expert in how to properly apply security controls (Figure 3.1).

A security engineer may also be involved with development projects in a larger organization. They may identify vulnerabilities in production applications, be part of a DevSecOps program, or provide stage gate reviews during a development project. But security engineers may also develop and provide solutions for security challenges within an organization. In larger security programs, security engineers might be building security tools or automating manual tasks. This field is still relatively new, and the description of the job role is changing quickly.

Even in smaller organizations, with the need to create and mature cybersecurity programs, security engineers are a natural solution. They are highly technical, familiar with a wide range of technology and tools, and can grow within the company as projects evolve and in-house development becomes more common. Security engineers, like security assessors/auditors must be able to work well together with other teams. In smaller organizations, they may need to collaborate with IT operations teams and management. But in a larger organization they might work with developers, other systems owners, network engineers, leads and management, as well as auditors and assessors.

But security engineers may be taking on the full load of security work in an organization. This means they may be responsible for the implementation

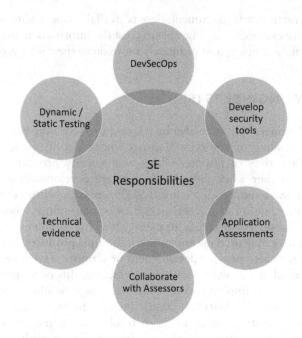

Figure 3.1 SE responsibilities.

and management of security tools, technical evidence for audits and assessments, working with systems owners to resolve vulnerabilities, continuous monitoring activities, and even IR. All these responsibilities can lead to early burn out, disgruntled employees, and lack of communication and coordination with other teams. And if these engineers are also responsible for projects and working with developers, they can be easily overworked and frustrated.

SECURITY MANAGERS (SMs)

Security Managers (SMs), or security team leads and management, are responsible for a wide range of security activities. They may work under a Chief Information Security Officer, the Chief Information Officer, or even directly for the Chief Executive Officer. These managers would be required to report on security incidents, coordinate security assessments for systems, as well as keep projects on track for security engagements. They may or may not have a technical background in security and have a business or management focused degree.

For a security management position, the individual must be highly organized, detailed, and efficient when working with multiple teams up and down the organization. Understanding the specialized applications, software, and intricacies of the environment play into successful implementation, construction, and development of systems. They must be strategic and coordinated in decision-making and can involve the right people at the right time. This type of pressure would be seen whether in a small or large organization but could be more challenging in highly complex environments.

A security manager must also be familiar with the laws, regulations, or frameworks to follow within their industry. For some organizations, must be familiar with the NIST RMF, Cybersecurity Framework, FeDRamp, and many other NIST guides like the 800-53 series. For the private sector, security managers may need to understand Payment Card Industry Data Security Standard, the General Data Privacy Regulation, and other privacy laws either locally, regionally, or globally. So, they must be able to understand technical requirements, security implications, and relevant regulations and laws.

A lack of understanding for laws and regulations could put an organization at risk for fines, at a bare minimum. Without the knowledge of associated laws and security frameworks, audits may fail, or the company could be at risk of lawsuit if they provide services to customers. But having this knowledge only goes so far – the manager must also be able to communicate those requirements and be aware of potential issues as they arise. Older systems may not meet current requirements, and new systems may need to go through rigorous testing and analysis to ensure they meet standards before putting into a production environment.

SECURITY ARCHITECTS

Security architects may have started careers on either the IT helpdesk or as a security analyst in an SOC. An architect would need a wide range of experience with IT infrastructure to understand how the various tools and technology work together, but also how to secure them. This knowledge must provide a balance between functionality and security and align with the business goals and strategy. Like engineers, security architects must understand the technical implications of security controls, but also how those changes align with the business. An architect may have held several positions within IT or security teams and are considered experts in their field.

An architect would be responsible for understanding large-scale and incredibly complex challenges. They must consider the current implementation of technology within the company, as well as how new products may better suit the needs of the business. They are constantly evaluating the security posture of a network and considering how large-scale changes would impact the organization. An architect must also be involved in the evaluation of new applications or infrastructure changes. A security architect can guide a project to make sure that whatever new technology is brought in, they are being done in a secure manner. This means understanding what access software will need, who would need permissions, what permissions, what ports must be open between other software, and what controls must be put in place to protect the infrastructure.

Security architects may exist in more medium to large-sized businesses, as an organizations' IT infrastructure becomes more complex. An architect may work with security engineers on development projects, or with business executives to help determine the best course of action for security issues across the enterprise. They may be responsible for building architecture diagrams, understanding the overall design of the IT environment, and providing guidance and recommendations for improving overall security. They may also help with security incidents or vulnerability remediation activities with large implications to the business. An architect may have security certifications, like the CISSP-ISSAP (Information Systems Security Architecture Professional), or have certifications that are product-specific, like an AWS Solutions Architect certification.

An architect must be able to understand highly complex security problems within the tech stack and translate that information across an organization. They must work well with executive management, engineers, SOC analysts, and IT operations and engineering teams. To properly secure an organization, they would need to build relationships and provide technical guidance independent of where the issue is within the tech stack. The communication skill for architects based on their need to understand complex problems and translate them up, down, and across an organization.

RED TEAMS

One of the most popular types of roles within cybersecurity is a red teamer, ethical hacker, or penetration tester. While this role may have a variety of names, the job responsibilities are similar in there are within cybersecurity. Red teams may be internal or external and are mostly focused on conducting technical tests of an environment to find vulnerabilities and exploit them. The main goal of an ethical hacker is to find vulnerabilities and document them for the organization, or customer, in order to provide a remediation or 'get well' plan. This 'get well' plan will provide an itemized list or report, which details the remediation details for each exploited vulnerability.

A red teamer's main concerns are to find creative ways of exploiting vulnerabilities, so they must be aware of and able to perform common types of attacks. An ethical hacker would be trained in common types of attacks and most often is a hands-on technical SME. An internal red team would focus on organizations own assets, and at larger companies the team may perform on-demand tests for known vulnerabilities, as well as engagements on special projects. An external red team can be employed to conduct penetration tests and simulate an external attack, with the same goals in mind.

They would conduct a penetration test after Rules of Engagement have been discussed.

A penetration tester must have in-depth knowledge of cyberattacks, understand, and employ the hacker methodology, as well as write technical reports for remediation steps. While a red team may not work directly with blue teams, or network defenders like SOC analysts, they are more successful when they are able to communicate effectively to blue teams. Whether internal or external, red teams and blue teams working in combination have been shown to increase time from finding and exploiting vulnerabilities, to resolving them (Poston, 2018). The collaboration between red and blue teams is known as purple teams, and they have a feedback loop between penetration test results from red teams and follow up remediation actions from the blue teams.

But this is a highly technical space, and unlike other roles within cybersecurity, red teams do not necessarily communicate across the organization in the same way. They may need to work with systems owners or administrators to understand technical features within an environment or gain access, but not necessarily how the environment works overall. Red teams may focus more on testing and report writing than being dependent on communication with other teams. This is not exclusive to every red team, but they are not usually in an operations or engineering capacity. They may focus more on red team engagements with customers or working with blue teams to provide vulnerability exploit findings.

INCIDENT RESPONSE

Cybersecurity analysts, engineers, or architects that work on an IR team may be seen more in larger organizations. Smaller businesses may have security analysts who are responsible for continuous monitoring, IR, network defense, and other tasks. But medium to large size organizations, who may be bigger targets for highly sophisticated attacks, may have dedicated IR teams. IR teams are comprised of analysts and engineers who monitor and manage security tools, as well as have an on-call rotation to respond to incidents. An IR analyst is trained in the IR methodology, just as an ethical hacker would need to learn the hacker methodology.

A cybersecurity incident may occur because of a phishing attack, Advanced Persistent Threat targeted attack, Denial of Service, or a variety of other types of attacks. An IR analyst must be able to find and determine common and innocuous attacks versus the very serious and advanced types of attacks that lead to full system compromise. As seen in several public data breaches, it can take anywhere from hours to months to detect an incident, and there is a lot of maturity that still needs to be done in the IR field (Figure 3.2).

An incident responder may come from a security analyst or engineering position, or may be on an IR team independent from the SOC. They may

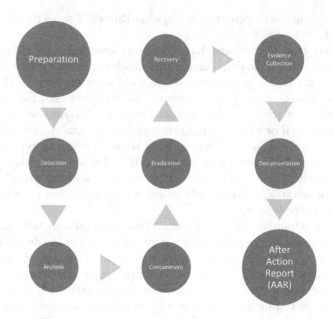

Figure 3.2 IR methodology diagram.

also be part of an on-call rotation for if an incident is detected off-hours. IR teams must be verse in common types of attacks, but not like a penetration tester, they must be able to detect and stop an incident from occurring. They must also understand how to contain a threat, versus shutting down a network and potentially losing forensics data. They must have excellent decision-making skills, be highly technical, and the ability to communicate serious and complex issues very quickly.

When an incident is actively occurring, these are the analysts and engineers that an organization can count on to identify and contain the threat. However, this is also a highly stressful position in that, in the past, IR teams have been blamed for attacks. This is a false belief in most instances; the IR team is there to identify the attack and were not the individuals who applied patches and security controls to systems. This type of role may require in-depth technical analysis of the incident, including the identification, containment, and remediation of the incident. More than likely, IR analysts and engineers would need to be highly technical and able to write lengthy reports and write-ups on incidents.

DIGITAL FORENSICS

Digital forensics is a field that spans outside of IT and development organizations and is used in numerous types of assessments and investigations.

Forensics work is conducted during and after investigations into user mis-use, possible insider threat issues, as well as IR within an organization. Digital forensics specialists' focus is on collecting and preserving data which may be used to determine how an incident occurred, who may be responsible for data loss, and may other use cases. Digital forensics is more recently closely associated with IR, and when the fields are combined, it is known as Digital Forensics/Incident Response, or DFIR.

Digital forensics experts understand the very core of each layer within an OS, an application, or a browser, and how to pull and store information. For example, a digital forensics expert may be called upon to determine if a user is downloading and removing information from a network. They may remotely access a users' machine to review time stamps on data down-loads, and may even be able to determine if the data was removed or exfil-trated from a system. This data would help an organization to catch insider threats, or potential malicious insiders. This forensics information could also be used to understand when a user is misusing company resources and the company can take the evidence to determine how they want to handle the situation (Figure 3.3).

A digital forensics expert is responsible for ensuring evidence is collected, stored, and processed appropriately, as this data may even be used in a criminal or civil case. If the forensics information is from an investigation into an insider threat case, without the proper handling of evidence, it may not be able to be used in the case. This could mean a case could be thrown

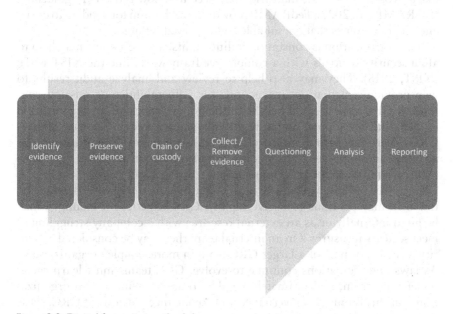

Figure 3.3 Digital forensics methodology.

out of court, the individual not convicted, or the organization may lose money and the data from such an incident. So digital forensics experts have a responsibility to understand the proper care and considerations for handling data which may be used as evidence.

This field is also important when considering how digital forensics work within an organization. For the most part, a forensics expert may be kept siloed from other groups within the business. This is because their work is primarily done either in secret or done quietly when trying to gather information on a case. They may also work closely with IR teams, and maybe even with systems administrators or SOCs when there is an incident or data breach. They may be brought in to collect and preserve evidence when trying to determine what type of attacker it was, when the attack occurred, and how many systems were compromised.

GOVERNANCE, RISK, AND COMPLIANCE

Governance, Risk, and Compliance, also known as GRC, is a newer field within cybersecurity that encompasses a wide range of skills. Primarily, the focus is on laws, risk management, and associated compliance frameworks. As cybersecurity becomes a more widely regulated field, experts in GRC are needed more to help organizations understand what laws and regulations apply to them. Governance needs are different based on location, within and outside the United States, for example organizations that develop products and would like to work with specific industries may need to follow FedRAMP guidelines (FedRAMP.gov, 2022). FedRAMP provides a mechanism for vendors to create and secure products that are suitable and approved for use.

If an organization is constantly failing audits, a GRC expert may help to align security controls with a compliance framework, like the NIST RMF (NIST, 2018). They may also help to review and analyze audit results to help provide remediation instructions for vulnerabilities or missing controls. A GRC expert could help with the policy aspects of an organization as well, like developing, updating, or enhancing a System Security Plan. A GRC expert may help to improve security policy, help an organization pass an audit, and improve security control implementation across an enterprise (Murray and Ward, 2018) (Figure 3.4).

Since GRC is still a relatively newly identified field within cybersecurity, this field may continue to evolve rapidly. GRC experts, for example, may be hired internally or as an external resource with a company struggling to meet security measures. On an internal team they may be considered a security assessor, or part of a larger GRC team in more complex organizations. As laws and regulations continue to evolve, GRC teams must learn them, understand them, and ultimately be able to apply them into an organization. But this is only the governance and compliance portions of GRC, these experts must also understand risk management.

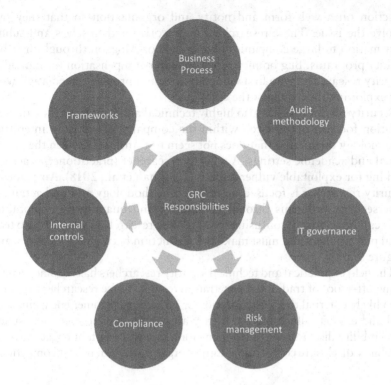

Figure 3.4 Diagram of GRC responsibilities (laws/frameworks).

The risk management component of GRC is mostly focused on frameworks, policies, and decision-making for the business. While there are several risk management frameworks available, the GRC expert must adapt them to their business. For example, a finance organization would not consider and accept risk in the same way that a private sector organization would. And even as a subset of risk management, organizations may use the terminology High Valued Asset (HVA) and treat HVA's risk differently than a standalone system that is not connected to a production network (CISA, n.d.). Risk management activities span the full people, process, and technology within any organization.

SECURITY RESEARCHERS

Security researchers are a specialty within cybersecurity, and these are not necessarily academic researchers. There are two types of security researchers, external and solo individuals who find and share exploit information with organizations. For example, they may find an exploitable SQL injection on a web form and notify and organization so that they may resolve the issue. These researchers may work for themselves and submit information to large companies like Google or Amazon through their bug bounty programs. Bug bounty programs offer compensation for individual security researchers who find vulnerabilities and provide remediation without exploiting them against the company.

Security researchers are also highly technical and may be part of an organization focused on research within the company. There is an interesting terminology distinction that does not seem to translate between the professional and academic settings. A security researcher (practitioner) is actively looking for exploitable vulnerabilities (Dadkhah et al., 2018). An academic security researcher is focused on research methodology and understanding cybersecurity problems through qualitative and quantitative exploration. This can be relatively confusing for academic researchers who are also technical practitioners and must make the distinction between types of research (Figure 3.5).

The field of practical and technical security researchers has become an interesting off-shoot of traditional penetration testing. These researchers are more than likely external to an organization or providing customer engagements to find and exploit vulnerabilities. If they are working alone, they may submit vulnerability disclosures to a company for a monetary sum or engage in a vulnerability disclosure competition. Larger organizations may host competitions

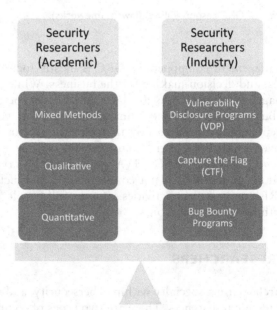

Figure 3.5 Difference between security researchers venn diagram.

to see who can find the most vulnerabilities and report them to the company for a prize. This is wildly different from what academic security researchers are doing within institutions or as part of a Research and Development group.

Academic security researchers primarily follow the scientific method to determine problems, identify hypothesis, gaps in current literature, and conduct experiments to understand phenomenon. These researchers may publish peer-reviewed research, create tools or applications based on experiments, or develop frameworks and taxonomies to resolve complex cybersecurity problems. But this is where the first issues are noted between technical practitioners and academic researchers. Security researchers who are exploiting vulnerabilities may not even be aware that there are academic researchers working at institutions to solve similar problems.

THREAT INTELLIGENCE ANALYSTS

Threat intelligence analysts are a specialist group within the cybersecurity industry. Their primary goal is to understand what intelligence exists within and outside an organization, related to threats and possible security concerns. They may be focused on using Open-Source Intelligence techniques to understand the Tactics, Techniques, and Procedures used by threat actors (Samtani et al., 2020). This field used to be relatively small at larger organizations, but more organizations in the private sector have their own threat intelligence groups. These groups may provide internal threat intelligence and hunting exercises or perform this type of analysis for a customer to determine what threats are most pertinent.

For example, a threat intelligence analyst working in the financial industry would focus on different threats than someone working in the energy sector. Analysts may use a variety of open-source or industry tools to collect information on types of attacks, threat actors who are actively exploiting vulnerabilities, or understanding the current threat landscape within an organization. These analysts can ingest a large amount of data and sort through disparate information to identify patterns and prioritize threats. They are integral in finding the latest types of threats and methods of attack within the industry, and the need for analysts has grown in recent years.

These threat intelligence analysts are more on the predictive and proactive side of cybersecurity. They are looking for trends or emerging threats based on types of technology and industry. They are on the forefront of finding and reporting these new threats across the industry. Analysts may be writing report to management or working with SOC teams when a threat is identified. They also provide advice on ports to monitor, network traffic that may be suspicious, or types of files to search the environment for to look for malicious items. Threat analysts work most closely with management and SOC teams to provide information.

Threat intelligence analysts must be able to identify anomalous or malicious trends in a large amount of data. They must also be versed in the latest threat intelligence tools and techniques used by malicious actors. Analysts must also be excellent communicators and effective writers for threat intelligence reporting. Communicating current threats is usually a critical activity and without a timely report, could lead to a data breach or system compromise. Writing reports is also critical to communicate with the general population or customers on what trends to monitor for in security tools.

CONCLUSION

Cybersecurity is a broad field with an ever-changing landscape of new roles, tools, and processes. From threat intelligence analysts to security researchers, engineers, architects, and SOC analysts, cybersecurity is changing quickly. As with the IT industry, there are so many new tools, techniques, and applications, and all of them require a unique security approach. There was an older mentality that people had about working in cybersecurity, that it was one type of job within an organization. But through learning about each of these separate roles, it is apparent how broad and how necessary it is to have different cybersecurity roles and skills.

As with IT roles, cybersecurity changes as technology changes. And as the technology changes these individuals must adapt and communicate effectively within and outside of their teams. Without proper communication, IT and cybersecurity teams are not able to perform their jobs effectively. They may be missing security controls, unable to identify possible gaps between technology and process, or work well with other teams. Cybersecurity personnel especially have a difficult time working with other groups, because of the mentality that they are only available to inhibit progress.

But this is simply not true. Cybersecurity professionals typically want to work in the industry because of a serious interest and calling to help organizations be more secure. Whether they come from a technical or academic background, cybersecurity professionals aim to improve security. This includes communicating positively and collaborating with a wide variety of teams within an organization. One bad interaction could lead to insecure configurations and failed IT projects. Management interaction between IT and cybersecurity teams adds another layer of complexity and the need to be able to articulate complex problems up and down the organization.

REFERENCES

CISA (n.d.). CISA insights: Security high value assets (HVAs). Retrieved from https://www.cisa.gov/sites/default/files/publications/CISAInsights-Cyber-SecureHighValueAssets_S508C.pdf.

Dadkhah, M., Lagzian, M., & Borchardt, G. (2018). Academic information security researchers: Hackers or specialists? *Science and Engineering Ethics*, 24, 758–790.

FedRAMP (2021). FedRAMP plan of actions and milestones (POA&M) template completion guide. Retrieved from https://www.fedramp.gov/assets/resources/documents/CSP_POAM_Template_Completion_Guide.pdf

FedRAMP (2022). How to become FedRAMP authorized. Retrieved from https://www.fedramp.gov/

Murray, P. J., & Ward, R. J. (2018). *Promoting Enterprise Risk Management (ERM) and Governance, Risk and Compliance (GRC) for Managing Cybersecurity Risks*. University of Maryland, Baltimore.

NIST (2011). SP 800-137. Information security continuous monitoring (ISCM) for federal information systems and organizations. Retrieved from https://nvlpubs.nist.gov/nistpubs/Legacy/SP/nistspecialpublication800-137.pdf

NIST (2018). SP 800-37 Rev. 2. Risk management framework for information systems and organizations: A system life cycle approach for security and privacy.doi:10.628/NIST.SP.800-37r2. Retrieved from https://csrc.nist.gov/publications/detail/sp/800-37/rev-2/final

Poston, H. (2018). How red teaming and blue teaming complement each other. Retrieved from https://resources.infosecinstitute.com/topic/how-red-teaming-and-blue-teaming-complement-each-other/

Richardson, R., & North, M. M. (2017). Ransomware: Evolution, mitigation and prevention. *International Management Review*, 13(1), 10–21.

Samtani, S., Abate, M., Benjamin, V., & Li, W. (2020, June). Cybersecurity as an industry: A cyber threat intelligence perspective. *The Palgrave Handbook of International Cybercrime and Cyberdeviance*. doi:10.1007/978-3-319-78440-3_8.

Chapter 4

Where IT meets cybersecurity

TECHNOLOGY MEETS CYBERSECURITY

The two previous chapters explored the variety of roles and teams within IT and cybersecurity departments. It is important to note that those fields are not all-encompassing and will evolve even at the time of this writing. However, the basis of both fields is rooted in how organizations use and function with technology. Most organizations cannot function without technology, they must have mobile devices, tablets, and a cloud infrastructure (of some kind) to keep up with changing markets and align with the business strategy.

The technology in use must function, and in larger organizations, it must function at a high level, with layers of high availability. This means that any cybersecurity strategy that exists within an organization must align with the operations and availability of the systems for internal and/or external users. For example, for any network architecture, security must apply controls and mitigations cautiously as any downtime could result in loss of revenue. Therefore, cybersecurity teams have historically had small budgets and smaller teams, because organizations focused their time and money more toward IT infrastructure or product development. With the onslaught of ransomware and software supply chain attacks, this older view of cybersecurity teams is starting to change (Figure 4.1).

Cloud systems, network management, and infrastructure hardware and software are all susceptible to cyberattacks. This means that each system must have its own secure configuration settings, which is one of the initial ways that cybersecurity meets IT. When deploying new servers, they should have a secure baseline configured before deployment, which may be set in policies or within an image. These servers may also require vulnerability scanning, antivirus, or Endpoint Detection and Response agents to enhance security monitoring and remediation activities. This is where some of the contention between IT and cybersecurity teams starts, operations groups may be more focused on quick deployments to meet business needs, whereas cyber teams are interested in implementing security measures from the start of a project.

Another area where IT and cybersecurity meet is when new frameworks or guidance are available from organizations/institutions like National

DOI: 10.1201/9781003264422-4

Newer Cyber Teams

• Threat Intelligence
• Emerging Technology
• Updated frameworks
• Security engineering practices
• Data Privacy concerns

Older Cyber Teams

• Security assessments
• Information Assurance
• Detection (A/V)
• Digital Forensics

Figure 4.1 Old cyber teams vs newer teams.

Institute of Technology and Standard (NIST), MITRE, or Carnegie Mellon. Frameworks like the Risk Management Framework (RMF) and the Cybersecurity Framework (CSF) exist to provide guidance for how to handle the cybersecurity and risk management lifecycles. NIST Special Publications, like the 800-53 series, also provide a grouping of security controls to apply to systems to harden or secure them at higher levels. To add even more complexity, depending on the industry that these systems exist, there may also be legal or alternate mandates which must be followed. For example, within the financial industry, they may be required to follow PCI-DSS (PCI Security Standards Council, n.d.) rules and regulations. Since cybersecurity and privacy laws are constantly evolving to ensure organizations are following basic security measures, this is a moving target.

Cybersecurity and IT programs also meet within the boots on the ground teams within IT and development and Security Operations Centers (SOCs). SOCs manage and monitor for alerts, malicious network traffic, or Indicators of Compromise. IT operations groups are monitoring server and network health, cloud infrastructure policies and deployment settings, as well as any other management or customer objectives. Developers are working to create new products, update and resolve bugs, and manage current deployments. Developers are also on the cutting edge of new technology and constantly re-evaluating what they are doing with new languages, development syntax, and improved functionality.

PEOPLE, PROCESS, AND TECHNOLOGY

One of the most common phrases in organizations is aligning and understanding people, process, and technology. While it was coined in the 1960s, it seems to be making a comeback at the time of this writing. This is mostly because organizations must align these three components to create a successful business. People, clearly, refers to the individuals who work within the organization. This spans HR departments, financial groups, IT and operations, development, data scientists, and cybersecurity teams. The people may also refer to third-party vendors, customers, partners, and other groups that work with an organization.

Process is related to the way that the organization operates. Standard Operating Procedures, or SOPs, are a common occurrence in any group within an organization. For example, an IT operations group may have an SOP for how to deploy Windows desktops using a tool. There could also be an SOP for how to create a baseline for that Windows desktop or package. Processes may also refer to how individuals are hired, how the company operates during holidays, or how user accounts are disabled or removed after an individual leaves the organization. These processes are the basis for how an organization handles day-to-day operations, as well as in the case of an emergency or incident. They are also more than likely documented and distributed widely to employees.

The technology aspect of this concept is becoming more complex every minute. From on premise data centers, to cloud native deployments, and hybrid cloud environments, complexity is the best way to describe it. Without a background in IT or operations, it is still clear to see how much systems have changed and adapted to current business needs. Users need to be mobile, access their tools, emails, and documents from a variety of devices, and have unique business requirements. With the increased telework presence over the last few years, it is essential for businesses to adapt and embrace new types of technology. Technology could mean anything from a physical device, like a tablet, to Infrastructure as Code or other types of cloud infrastructure. This could also refer to networking equipment, serverless infrastructure, financial software like QuickBooks, or anything in between.

Of note, each of these three categories has become increasingly complex, and there are no signs of simplifying any time soon. Processes are comprehensive and constantly changing to keep pace with business strategy and new partnerships, new laws, regulations, as well as new data released about workplace safety, to name a few. Processes are typically living documents, which means they are updated monthly, weekly, or even daily. These processes, if not outlined or developed well, could lead to confusion and even lawful action if they do not align with current laws and regulations. An example would be a process for handling incidents within the incident response team. The incident reporting process may be dependent on several groups, including chains of communication, and updated information for new and different types of attacks. A malware incident would certainly be handled separately from a ransomware attack.

Technology has also been changing so quickly that many organizations may be missing updating processes, documentation, or cybersecurity to align with new and emerging technology. The hope is that someday, technology will be required to implement security in the design process, instead of leaving it up to the user, developer, or deployment teams. But until then, technology, tools, and code are not necessarily required to be created securely. This means security may be an additional component and another component that needs to be considered for developers and operations groups. Any organization that has been around for some time will have a complex infrastructure, legacy applications, End of Life (EOL) equipment, and may be working to integrate new technology into their current environment. This adds layers and layers of intricacy and relationships between software and hardware that increase difficulty in maintaining and managing said environments.

PEOPLE

The **people** component deserved its own section from the people, process, and technology concept. The state of different types of individuals within organizations has evolved as quickly as the technology they use. Technology and cybersecurity objectives weave throughout the people of an organization. In IT or cyber we call the people that consume technology, users, or administrators. It is more common to discuss the people in the type of role they have or the permissions that are assigned to them. This can sometimes remove the human element of how IT and cyber professionals view concerns or issues with experience or incidents. There can be a tendency to use terms like 'stupid user' or 'IBCAK', and 'Issue Between Chair and Keyboard'.

This type of view can be harmful to understanding how users work, their challenges, and what may eventually lead to a data breach or cybersecurity attack. Even as of 2021, phishing attacks comprised 43% of successful data breaches, and 75% of U.S. organizations experienced some sort of phishing attack Rosenthal (2022). These phishing attacks ultimately target users of any variety, and through a multitude of different techniques, but with the goal of dropping malware, ransomware, or compromising accounts. So, this should change the way we think about users, back into the people who consume and use this technology to complete their work within an organization. Individuals within companies may be responsible for data breaches or cyberattacks, and without proper empathy or understanding, it may be difficult to fully understand the challenges that lead to these cyberattacks.

People may occupy many roles within an organization, as a recruiter, data scientist, researcher, executive, administrative assistant, developer, engineer, architect, and the list goes on. Each job, of course, comes with its own responsibilities, duties, and expertise to align with the business. But from a technology perspective, it is more common that an IT or cyber professional would be

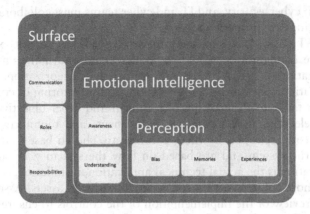

Figure 4.2 Diagram of complexity of people within org.

aware of the types of software users require and utilize daily. For example, a statistician, analyst, or data scientist may use tools such as R Studio or Tableau. From an IT perspective, the user may be identified by the types of software they use and associated patches or configuration settings. From a cybersecurity perspective, the user may be identified more by any alerts seen in the SOC or evaluation of software for security concerns (Figure 4.2).

There may also be vendors, third-party contacts, or contractors that are considered part of an organization. They may have restricted access or may be part of the organization's domain or IAM solution. These users may require special access to data or need to collaborate with specific people. This also adds to the risk management concerns for the cybersecurity team. IT teams may need to understand permissions and data access points, which would incorporate communication and potentially consultation with the cyber team. Another example of where technology meets cybersecurity, through the people within the organization. While these examples are only a few of the potential interactions or technical considerations, IT and cybersecurity teams must collaborate throughout the people of the organization.

SECURE CONFIGURATION

Secure configuration is another example of where IT and cybersecurity objectives meet and must be considered thoughtfully. Secure configuration is the implementation of security controls, policies, or settings, to secure software or hardware. These settings or controls may be group policies within Active Directory (AD), configuration to lock down publicly available S3 buckets in Amazon Web Services deployments, or creation of a secure baseline for Windows OS desktops. Secure configuration is a massive area within cybersecurity, and IT and cyber teams must collaborate well to ensure settings are properly in place.

The NIST Risk Management Framework (RMF) is a great example of how secure configuration would be implemented and maintained within an organization (NIST, 2018). RMF outlines the categorization, selection, implementation, assessment, authorization, and monitoring of controls. Of most importance to the meeting of technical and cyber objectives are the areas of selection, implementation, assessment, and monitoring. Within the framework, selection is where controls are chosen based on their relevance to the system and are based on how the system was categorized. Implementation is the actual technical application, installation, or incorporation of those controls within software or hardware assets. Assessment is the initial review of the implementation of the controls to ensure that they were applied properly. And finally, monitoring is the ongoing review of the technical controls to ensure they are kept in place as agreed upon by the IT and cyber teams.

Cyber teams are possibly responsible for the selection of security controls, but more often involved with the assessment and monitoring of controls. Security teams may be involved during the onset of an IT project to provide guidance for which security controls should be implemented based on their expertise or legal requirements for the system. For assessments, a security analyst or may provide initial review of the security tools with a vulnerability scanner and provide a report to the IT team for confirmation that the controls were set properly. This assessment may be done before deploying new OS baselines, new applications, or reviewing code before it is deployed to production. Cyber teams also continuously monitor these controls with daily, weekly, or monthly scans to ensure the controls are still in place. If controls are found to be removed or not functioning as expected, security teams will reach out to the system owner to understand why the control was removed or determine if there is another issue within the system.

IT teams are primarily responsible for the selection and implementation of secure configuration settings. The selection process may be done in combination with cyber teams, to ensure that the chosen controls align with business and risk management strategies. This selection of controls would be based on how the system was categorized, how the system will be used, and what access the system may need. For example, a system that is publicly available would be treated differently than one that is standalone. The technical implementation of controls is also dependent on what type of system is being developed or updated. The implementation by an IT team may be a new group policy, might be the creation of a Windows 11 OS baseline for desktop deployments, or what permissions users will have in HR versus the Finance department.

But IT and cyber teams must collaborate on all aspects of the incorporate of secure configuration and baselines within the organization. Without this partnership, IT teams may select improper controls, implement them without a full assessment, or have insecure configurations found during monitoring activities that may ultimately create tension between the teams. These insecure configurations are constantly a concern on the Open Web Application Security Project (OWASP) Top 10 lists (OWASP, 2021). Without the proper controls in place, business proprietary data may be leaked, or a full system compromise could be possible by a malicious actor. Even one bad interaction between IT and cyber teams during the implementation of controls could lead to a devastating cyberattack.

RISK MANAGEMENT

Risk management is a large and broad concept, and carries many definitions, depending on where you sit within an organization. Risk management is the coordinated activities used to direct and manage activities regarding risk (Hopkin, 2018). As mentioned in the previous section, the NIST RMF helps to identify and monitor risk throughout the enterprise using the framework. Risk may be accepted, rejected, mitigated, or transferred based on how the organization sees fit for each situation. For example, a system that is used by customers may be deemed high risk because if it is not operational, it would cost the business revenue.

IT groups may be more concerned about risk management from an operations or business functionality perspective. If an application contains a bug that does not allow customers to choose an option from a checkout of an online store, that may take priority over other configurations or issues. Because that bug may cause inability for customers to choose items or purchase as many objects as they would like, affecting revenue for the company. If email services are down for the organization, this may impact how executives communicate with each other, their teams, or even partners and board members. An outage affecting email would be of the utmost priority for IT teams as it affects VIP members, which again, ultimately may affect revenue and sales.

Cyber teams may consider risk management from a different angle than their IT counterparts. Risk management may be more focused on how much data may be exposed to the public if a specific control is not in place. Or risk may mean how much a threat actor is likely to exploit a vulnerability if it goes unpatched or unresolved. Risk might also speak to how concerned the SOC is by a specific spike in network traffic to a country that is considered anomalous behavior. Cyber analysts and engineers consider risk more from the perspective of what may happen if a setting is not in place, alerts are not managed or reviewed, or vulnerabilities are not remediated. This view of risk is disparate between IT and cyber teams and may cause discord or misunderstanding because the goal of risk management is quite different for each team (Figure 4.3).

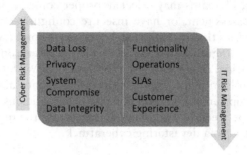

Figure 4.3 Where it and cyber disagree on risk.

IT and cyber teams may understand and treat risk in competition, instead of aligning their objectives. Without cohesion of risk management activities, IT teams may ignore cybersecurity advice, and cyber teams may get frustrated with the lack of security understanding on IT teams. The inability to effectively communicate risk, or understand that their objectives may be separate, and even competing at times, leads to insecure configuration. For example, if an IT team does not take a recommendation from a security group to apply a network setting, the security team may raise the issue to management for review. Once management is involved, this could lead to further discord between the teams, because the IT group could be under increased scrutiny by their leads or executive sponsors.

However, if IT and cybersecurity teams work together early and often, most of the conflict may be resolved. Take, as an example, an IT project begins without the consultation or inclusion of a security team. The project is to build a new program to provide to data scientists to analyze larger sets of data. The program is designed and built without the incorporation of the security team. This product is then in final stages of review and leadership asks what security thinks of the deployment before entering production. Security teams find major concerns and risks with this program, to include passwords sent in clear text. But to remediate this finding, it may take the development team weeks or months to resolve the vulnerability and determine a new method of password management. Ultimately, this last-minute find could cost the organization money and resources to resolve if they had not just included security in the design process.

LEGAL AND PRIVACY CONCERNS

Privacy for personal information and data across the enterprise has become a major concern for several reasons and repercussions from newer cyberattacks. Privacy is a hot topic based on the new and evolving laws around data privacy and protection (Christen et al., 2020). And based on geolocation, privacy policies and programs may be regulated or mandated by law. Newer fields of privacy engineers and analysts are now part of the job role landscape. While not specifically addressed here, IT and cybersecurity teams will be interacting more and more with privacy engineers to ensure that security AND privacy regulations are met. This means the need for communications and collaboration between engineering, operations, security, and privacy teams.

And while these are new fields, cyber and IT teams may be operating without privacy engineers until it becomes a more prevalent field within the industry. This means that cyber and IT groups need to communicate and understand some serious terminology and language to be able to configure their systems accordingly. Without a basic understanding of how laws and regulations affect the products in use within the organization, technical teams may face failed audits, fines, or even loss of reputation if they are unable to meet regulations. Given the increased complexity of laws and regulations around cybersecurity requirements, the people, processes, and technology must align to be successful.

Privacy has become a hot topic for organizations, including the inclusion of privacy and data engineers and architects. Privacy programs are being developed and work closely with cybersecurity groups to align their goals and technology. This partnership is essential for organizations that handle customer data. This is also an international concern since each country is developing and requiring different components for their privacy regulations. It is essential the organizations consider how privacy and legal regulations will shape the future of their cybersecurity and IT programs.

DEVSECOPS

Development and operations groups have historically had difficulty working together. Developers build and update code and deploy it to the production where the operations group would classically handle tickets and issues. But this led to lots of issues because if the operations team was unsure how to resolve an issue, they would have to go back to the development team. This meant that there was an extra layer of communication required between users and developers, and the need to translate problems between teams. Operations teams are more focused on day-to-day maintenance, tasking, and resolving issues, whereas development teams are more focused on the actual code and integration of user functionality into the application.

This potential bottleneck led to the idea of DevOps – the integration of development and operations teams from day one of a project. Incorporating development and operations teams meant increased understanding of each other's objectives and needs when problems arose. And with DevOps, the concept of Agile, the ability to create, update, and manage code on a much faster development cycle. A very common method of development is using

2-week sprints for developing and updating code and pushing to production, versus the original method of development that could take a year from creation to production. Agile allows for teams to constantly iterate and resolve issues – break it fast, fix it fast.

While agility and constant iteration occurred between development and operations, one team was left out of the equation. Security groups may have been left to the end of a project, or only introduced when there was a potential security problem before deployment. Still a somewhat new concept, DevSecOps incorporates developers, security engineers, and operations teams into one group. This allows for open and constant communications between these teams to implement security from the onset of a project. With security shifting left in the production pipeline, both technical and security concerns can be found early and resolved quickly. No more delays to production because of a bad security assessment; by the time a product is ready for deployment, it should have been thoroughly tested and approved by security (Figure 4.4).

DevSecOps is the incorporation of functionality and security objectives, where before there may have been little to no interaction or understanding. And while DevSecOps may not be used in all projects, the idea behind it is the blending of technology and security. Instead of waiting for a final security assessment at the end of a project, security is given a seat at the project management table and able to provide consultation throughout development cycles. Security engineers are given a better understanding of the requirements of a project, development teams are able to ask questions and implement security early on, and operations group can learn about how security may impact the program. DevSecOps is a great example of how business objectives, technical functionality, and security measures can all meet harmoniously.

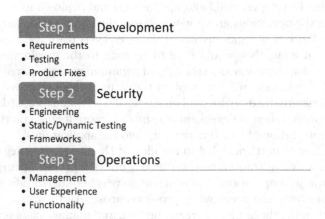

Figure 4.4 DevSecOps venn diagram.

ARCHITECTURE

Architecture is the enterprise-level design of IT or cybersecurity systems. An architect would have a 30,000-foot view of the enterprise, while still being incredibly technical and understanding a wide variety of tools and applications. Architects collaborate with upper-level management, operations teams, engineering groups, and vendors or third parties as they integrate with their systems. They are both highly technical and able to translate very complex problems into something easily digestible for any audience. A typical day may include building a cloud infrastructure diagram, working with systems owners to integrate new products into their environments, or working with management to acquire new technology.

An IT architect may work in a variety of teams and capacities, from network to cloud or platform architecture. They may help an organization move from an on-premises deployment to building a new environment in the cloud – to include how those systems would be integrated. An IT architect might also work with Identity and Access Management (IAM), network, and AD teams to solve complex problems in the environment. When there is a need for new technology, they may conduct Proof of Concepts or pilots to determine if the software would be appropriate for the environment. They would also need to work with security teams to ensure that the product/s they evaluate meet a certain standard.

A security architect would have very different goals, but may perform some of the same tasking. A security architect, unlike their IT counterparts, would be more focused on the integration of security measures during the onset of projects. They would also help to re-architect systems within the organization to implement security controls. For example, they may help to re-architect a Citrix environment if they found that there was no High-Availability, lack of data integrity measures in place, and lacking security controls on the associated network devices. More than likely, both IT and security architects would be on the same projects, or at least aware of each other's ongoing tasking. Security would need to be apprised of any new technology coming into the environment, and IT would need to know if security controls, or guidance was changing and what the impacts would be.

But IT and security architects do not just work together on new projects – they must work together when there are major security concerns noted in an environment. If a major vulnerability is found in several products, and executive management comes to the decision that it must be removed from the environment, architects may collaborate to identify new applications or technology that would fill that need. The IT and security architects would more than likely need to collaborate on major events like SolarWinds or Log4j, which may require upgrades, removal of software, or implementation of new security measures to mitigate the findings.

Without this collaboration between IT and security architects, or individuals who would be responsible for those tasks, projects fail. There is a running theme starting to emerge between teams who need to coordinate and collaborate on activities. Technical projects fail or may be delayed, programs may be missing critical security controls, and operations teams could be left in the dark when architects make decisions without understanding current environments. Anyone who is making decisions at an enterprise level regarding implementing new products and services needs to understand both technical and security implications.

NEW IT/DEVELOPMENT PROJECTS

Every organization has at least one ongoing IT-related project, whether it is implementing a new email system, moving to an Infrastructure as Code environment, or integrating new encryption methods on systems certificates. These projects require budgets, resources, skilled technicians and administrators, as well as careful planning and coordination. Some projects are easier and implemented quickly, like adding a new feature into a website or adding some functionality to a program. Others take more time and might affect other systems, like upgrading to new OS levels, migrating systems from physical to virtual, or moving services to a mobile infrastructure.

When a new technology is proposed, like a new virtual infrastructure for servers and desktops, several teams would get involved. While the project may be born of a need to save money or migrate away from legacy systems, there are many security implications. A new project like updating network equipment, if current configurations are not implemented properly, could lead to gaps in security controls. Or another example, creating new test servers in a cloud infrastructure and accidently leaving them open to the public.

Risk management is a big topic, but for the purposes of new projects, this is exactly where technology and security meet. Understanding risk to operations, user functionality, privacy, and security are all part of new IT projects. This is another area where the use of proper terminology and understanding common definitions can be an issue. Risk might mean being concerned about downtime for IT operations, whereas risk may be the ability for an attacker to exploit a vulnerability in a system for cybersecurity teams. In order to understand risk in new projects, teams should consider what it means to their own goals, as well as how risk may apply to other groups.

When a need for a new feature or program comes up from customer requirements or business need, this is a perfect spot for technology and security to meet. DevSecOps was discussed as the integration between developers, software engineers, and security groups (Pendyala, 2020). But the onset of a development project would include the management team, project managers, developers, security, and potentially customer engagement and design teams. In new development projects, security would need to understand the needs of developers, customers, and business strategy. This helps to ensure programs are developers to meet both functionality and security initiatives.

EMPATHY IN IT AND CYBERSECURITY

Empathy is not discussed nearly enough in IT and cybersecurity teams. Empathy is the ability to understand and comprehend another person's experience and emotions (APA, n.d.). There are many cases in organizations where a lack of empathy may lead to downtime or insecure configurations. It may also lead to disorganization, confusion, and inability to collaborate with other teams effectively. So why do organizations, teams, and individuals not discuss empathy or emotional intelligence? Emotional intelligence is a common leadership topic, so why not within operations, development, and cybersecurity teams?

IT teams, as discussed, are focused on customer functionality and operations tasks, while also potentially being concerned with closing tickets or working on projects. Even though IT teams collaborate with many other groups in an organization, they may not have a full understanding of how other teams operate. Many IT groups are overloaded with daily operations task, and the ability to collaborate or spend time working with other teams may be minimal. Even within massive organizations an email team may not need to work often with the AD team, so they may not even have a view into other IT groups. And their only interaction with security may be to receive vulnerability reports, they would not see how much times goes in to developing those reports. So, empathy from within IT groups, to other IT teams in larger organizations or cybersecurity groups, may be minimal.

Cybersecurity teams, likewise, may not understand the day-to-day operations within an IT team. If a security analyst or engineer has a background in IT operations, that would drastically change the amount of empathy available to understand what their daily tasking looks like. But without this background knowledge, a cybersecurity analyst may be frustrated or confused why an IT team has not resolved vulnerabilities within a timely manner. They may not understand the operations group is responding as quickly as they can, while also meeting customer and executive management requests.

A lack of empathy of understanding for other teams tasking and priorities could ultimately lead to lack of secure configuration. If a systems administrator is working on ten tickets, managing several systems, as well as working on projects for system upgrades, security may not be a focus for them. And when a security analyst comes to them and asks them why they have not remediated vulnerabilities, it may be too much for the administrator to handle. There may just be too much on their plate for them to handle daily tasks, and with just a report and no information on remediation from a security team, it becomes very challenging to collaborate well. In a worst-case scenario, the vulnerabilities would not be remediated for some time.

CONCLUSION

If it is not evident yet, IT and cybersecurity teams have different goals, objectives, and requirements for their teams. But while their missions may be different, they must meet in several ways to incorporate technical and security requirements, whether it is working on a new development project, understanding risk in the environment, or working through architecture diagrams. IT and cybersecurity team must collaborate to meet both groups' goals. Without understanding the complexity of issues facing IT and cybersecurity teams, they will not be able to reach their full potential of lowering risk and improving functionality of systems.

Organizations are constantly implementing new technology to increase their efficacy, revenue, and work more effectively. Groups must adapt quickly to this new technology, and without collaboration between IT and cybersecurity teams, technology will always be lagging. And while technology is an important component of to discuss, equally important are the people working on the implementation. Empathy, understanding, and compassion can help an IT project succeed, and this concept will be explored more in-depth in later chapters.

REFERENCES

APA (n.d.). Empathy. Retrieved from https://dictionary.apa.org/empathy.

Christen, M., Gordijn, B., & Loi, M. (2020). The ethics of cybersecurity. Springer Link.

Hopkin, P. (2018). *Fundamentals of Risk Management: Understanding, Evaluating and Implementing Effective Risk Management*. Martin P Hill Consulting, New York.

OWASP (2020). OWASP top ten. Retrieved from https://owasp.org/www-project-top-ten/.

PCI Security Standards Council (n.d.). Securing the future of payments together. Retrieved from https://www.pcisecuritystandards.org/.

Pendyala, V. (2020). Evolution of integration, build, test, and release engineering into devops and to DevSecOps. *IGI Global*. DOI: 10.4018/978-1-7998-1863-2. ch001

Rosenthal (2022). Must-know phishing statistics: Updated 2022. Retrieved from https://www.tessian.com/blog/phishing-statistics-2020/.

Chapter 5

The disconnect
(IT vs cybersecurity)

THE DISCONNECT

Understanding IT and cybersecurity professionals, their education and certifications, typical job roles and duties, as well as where technology and cyber lay the foundation for where problems and contention exist between teams. The major problem between IT and cybersecurity groups is the disconnect. While this topic has not been discussed within an organizational setting, it can lead to so many other problems and has a trickle-down effect in an organization. And not just from between IT and cybersecurity groups, but any discord or contention between these teams may also affect executive management, revenue, and other aspects of the organization. It is increasingly important to have this discussion so we can determine how far reaching these issues can be.

Discord between teams can start with something simple, like one bad interaction between co-workers. A vulnerability report was sent to a systems administrator which contains a list of 300 vulnerabilities, no organization or prioritization, no instructions sent with it. The administrator who received the report may be frustrated with the lack of guidance and organization to the report, or simply too busy to handle it. The administrator may not resolve the vulnerabilities, remediate a few of the Critical or High vulnerabilities, or send back the report and ask for more information. Each time a vulnerability is not remediated quickly, there is an opportunity for an attacker to exploit said vulnerability.

Because time is of the essence in remediation of security findings, any period spent sending emails back and forth to gain understanding or insight, could lead to days or weeks between identification and remediation. When considering how much time, there may also be other projects that come up in between that report being sent and receiving instructions. There could also be a security incident in that time, where those vulnerabilities may be pushed to the side and not remediated for extra weeks or even months. There may also be new products or tools that need to be integrated by the same IT group, which could take precedence based on executive leadership decisions.

DOI: 10.1201/9781003264422-5

This is one interaction, one point in time, for an interaction between one administrator and security analyst. Consider the amount of vulnerability scans conducted, vulnerabilities found, new IT projects and tools being added to environments. New processes, frameworks, guidelines, and laws may also complicate these interactions. And in larger organizations with different teams dedicated to specific tools, like a team for email and one for Public Key Infrastructure, the complexity grows in depth and breadth.

A HISTORY OF DISCORD

When organizations started to increasingly implement new types of technology and infrastructure to support their businesses, IT teams started to grow. But as is very much the case with current cybersecurity teams, IT groups were initially very small. Maybe a few helpdesk administrators, systems administrators or engineers, network engineers, and potentially someone in an architect-type role. The Chief Information Officer (CIO) may have had smaller teams initially, and Chief Technology Officer roles were scarce. Chief Information Security Officer (CISO) roles were seen more at larger organizations, but even early on there were very few holding that title.

While IT teams exploded with organizations increasingly focused on expanding their digital footprint, the required skills and types of IT professionals grew. CIOs had increasing responsibilities and were ultimately responsible for the business' success with technology. Now, implementing emerging technology is considered digital transformation, as well as moving to cloud infrastructure and using containers instead of physical servers and systems. So, IT teams must quickly adapt to new technology, as seen in previous sections. This meant that administrators and engineers had to up-skill quickly, with or without the support of the organization.

But as malware, trojans, worms, and other malicious types of attacks grew in ease of use for attackers, organizations realized the need for security. This meant that initially, IT teams had to learn how to secure their own environments, potentially without the aid of a security team. Security teams, originally, were more focused on physical controls and securing the hardware within a data center. As systems became more connected to the Internet (with the onset of Internet of Things devices), as well as more interconnected systems, security became more complex than the installation and management of antivirus and anti-malware tools (Figure 5.1).

As IT administrators and engineers were working to secure their environments, cybersecurity teams became more prevalent. This need was born of increased scrutiny on companies for their lack of security and privacy controls. While privacy is not a focus in this book, it is another emerging field that integrates with IT and security and adds to the complexity of team dynamics. There was also an increase in laws, regulations, and available frameworks for companies to use to create and develop their cybersecurity programs.

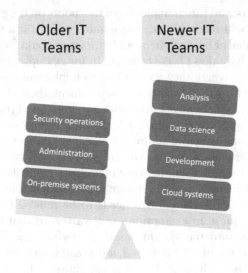

Figure 5.1 IT responsibilities: past vs present.

Now IT teams had to adapt to having another team imposing security controls and before more sophistication was available, most cybersecurity teams were sending vulnerability reports with little context.

This initial interaction between IT and cybersecurity teams may have been fraught with tension and misunderstanding, especially given the constantly changing technology landscape. CIOs were working with executive management and probably board members and investors to meet the changing business needs, while also increasingly being concerned with how security may affect their environments. Cybersecurity controls were initially done out of a necessity to satisfy audit requirements, meet expectations for basic security controls, or concern over how a cyberattack may impact business functionality. IT and cybersecurity teams had to shift quickly to how they would need to work together and address competing requirements.

FUNCTIONALITY

Functionality, operability, and consistency are all terms that are essential to an IT operating environment. Without functionality, the business may lose revenue and customers, or may be unable to keep up with competitors. Without appropriate functionality for employees and users, businesses would be unable to provide required services to the public. That could mean loss in functionality from delivering mail on time, accessibility of military records, or ability for law enforcement to work on criminal cases. Regardless of industry, without functionality, organizations and agencies are not able to meet their business goals.

IT teams understand functionality from the 'boots on the ground' perspective. A helpdesk will receive increasing number of calls if a service is down, potentially be yelled at by customers, and ultimately could face job loss if they make a mistake that takes IT assets down. If, for example, an IT administrator had a situation where they were asked to implement a security control, and it ended up taking down the entire environment, they would be very hesitant to implement more controls. And with good reason, if they were verbally warned, written up, or even put on a Performance Improvement Plan, they would be very cautious before adding more security to their systems.

And in a similar way, if adding layers of security affects the operability of system, IT administrators will be wary of security controls. For example, if a control is implemented and the system becomes unstable or slows down, the IT team may argue the control needs to be removed. Administrators and leads may request an exemption, or a waiver, so that the control will not be integrated into the system based on performance issues. While a temporary exemption may be required, it is possible that the control is never implemented, or is implemented far into the future. This leaves a potential gap in the system for an attacker to use, and the security team may not have provided a possible mitigating control in this situation.

One incredibly important note, these situations are hypothetical, but are all possible scenarios which may be occurring in the organization today. Without a full picture into what exemptions or waivers currently exist in an environment, it is difficult to say what level of security these systems achieve. Even though audits may require evidence of exemptions, waivers, or screenshots of security controls in place, this is an outside view of what the security landscape looks like. And, for example, if an IT administrator found that an initial security control caused problems, it is possible that in 2 or 3 months' time the control could be re-evaluated and introduced into the system.

IT groups will be more concerned with functionality than security, which is appropriate based on their job descriptions, skillsets, and management expectations. This will always be a top concern, and that does not need to change. IT groups exist for a reason – to keep the business running. But the discord between IT and cybersecurity teams does not exist because IT teams are fulfilling their job responsibilities, it is because of a lack of understanding and empathy for each other. It is human nature that we do not always see, or understand, someone else's perspective on a situation.

SECURITY

Cybersecurity teams exist for one reason – secure all the things. And securing an environment does not just mean installing and managing security tools, it means detection, response, and continuous monitoring of systems. Cybersecurity groups may still be very small in comparison to larger IT or development groups. Security assessors/auditors and Security Engineers (SEs) may be responsible for multiple different systems within large organizations. It is possible that even for environment of 10,000 employees, the cybersecurity team may be 10–20 people, including the CISO and management team. Whereas an IT group may have 50–60 people or more, to support that many users, and a development team may have 30–40 depending on how much in-house development the organization does.

These numbers are loosely based on how budgets may be aligned within an organization. Even at the time of this writing, cybersecurity budgets are much smaller than IT budgets. This means fewer resources, tools, and team members available to support the cybersecurity initiatives of an organization. Cybersecurity teams must be agile, contain a variety of skillsets, and adjust quickly to match their malicious counterparts. Cybersecurity teams must keep up with the latest trends in technology, while understanding the latest security frameworks, laws and regulations, new types of attacks, and continuous monitoring of their environment for potential malicious activity. All these responsibilities may fall on a very small team. This team must also collaborate with IT, developers, management, auditors, and third parties.

As cybersecurity teams' skillsets have changed over time, the focus stays the same, securing the environment and protecting against threats. While working with IT teams, developers, and other groups, security assessors/auditors and SEs may not initially understand the functionality and operability requirements of a system. They initially would work to implement security based on the project onset, audit findings, or vulnerability scans and reports to address missing controls. It is possible that security teams may also get involved during an incident and find other missing security controls or vulnerabilities to be addressed. And this may be where the discord begins because a security analyst may report a vulnerability to an IT administrator and could receive push back for implementing the control.

In contrast to IT teams, cybersecurity groups are responsible for the overall security of an environment. Although in a similar way, if the security of a network is compromised, it is possible that a security analyst or engineer would be held responsible for the breach. They may also face similar actions like a verbal/written warning or being placed on a Performance Improvement Plan. Security teams would put pressure on systems owners to remediate vulnerabilities and implement the proper security controls because ultimately, they want the systems to be secure. But security assessors/auditors and SEs do not always understand the IT functionality requirements or may not be as empathetic when receiving push back. This is another way that discord begins and may linger between IT and cybersecurity teams.

To understand how the discord, miscommunication, or disharmony began and persists between IT and cybersecurity groups, three scenarios are presented. The first scenario is from the focus of an IT operator/administrator that implemented a security control and it broke functionality within their system. The second is also from the perspective of both the IT administrator and security analyst when a report with 300 findings is involved. The third and final scenario is from the perspective of a security analyst who is working to resolve an exemption to a vulnerability finding for end-of-life (EOL) software. Each scenario will provide a different perspective, moment in time, and example of how problems can start between IT and cybersecurity teams.

IT VS CYBER: ROUND 1

One fine day, an IT administrator arrives at work to find an email from a security analyst. The email specifies a group policy change that must occur quickly to address a known vulnerability within the environment. Even though not too much detail is provided, there is enough information to understand the urgency and the technical requirements for the finding. As is Standard Operating Procedure, the administrator submits the change request to the Technical Review Board (TRB) for approval. The administrator also creates the new group policy with the setting and applies it to a development server for testing before implementation.

The initial tests show no issues with the development server, but there are limited tests available based on the number of users who interact with the server. The administrator can perform a few scenarios for general use on the server and determines there are no issues. At the weekly TRB meeting, the administrator provides initial findings and that this change must be made based on security requirements. The TRB approves the change and determines it will be made during the next maintenance window, which is every Friday morning between 4:00 and 7:00 am. The administrator wakes up early, logs in from home, and applies the group policy to all member servers, but is unable to reboot all of the servers within the maintenance window, meaning that some servers did not receive the change initially.

Since this is a change that requires a reboot to implement, during the business day on Friday, there do not appear to be any issues. But during the weekend, more servers are rebooted and early Monday morning, users start complaining about inability to log in to certain applications. Because the administrator does not know of any changes that took place over the weekend, it may take some time to troubleshoot the root cause. After a couple of hours of testing, while receiving emails from management and customers to determine what happened and that they are unable to work, they find that it was the group policy change that broke the systems. They disable the group policy and reboot appropriate servers to bring back functionality for users.

In the time it took to troubleshoot and resolve the issue, management has been asking for constant updates, the administrator has received multiple tickets from the helpdesk on the same issue, and customers have been calling to find out the status. It is possible they are feeling overwhelmed, frustrated,

Figure 5.2 Communication path – pinpoint the breakdown.

and stressed due to the situation, and may be blamed for not testing thoroughly before adding the group policy to production servers. But based on how many systems they manage, the number of hours they spend on maintenance and operations task alone, they may not have had a lot of time to research potential issues with the change. And without understanding the way the system functions, the security analyst who sent the email may not have known possible implication for the change (Figure 5.2).

The communication breakdown (shown above) led to a broken system, unhappy customers, and an IT administrator who may feel overwhelmed and frustrated with what transpired. The administrator may have received the angry end of management phone calls, emails, and visits to their desk for updates. Even though the security analyst had no way of knowing that the change would break the environment, the IT administrator may blame them for the change. This may begin a contentious relationship between the IT and cybersecurity teams because both sides of the argument would share their perspective of what happened. Teammates would naturally feel for their own group and would potentially be wary of future interactions with IT or cybersecurity groups.

IT VS CYBER: ROUND 2

This next scenario will be viewed from two different perspectives, from a systems engineer and a security assessor. The assessor has sent an email to the systems engineer with a list of 300 findings. These findings encompass the entire system and while they are organized by severity, and detail is provided for remediation within the report, it is still an excel spreadsheet with 300 individual findings. The systems engineer received this report and was told only that the items would need to be remediated, and the assessor did offer to meet with them to understand and help prioritize the items. The findings include both software and platform vulnerabilities, as well as security controls missing based on the NIST SP 800-53 series (Figure 5.3).

Vulnerability	Systems Affected	Due Date
SQL Injection (9.0 - Critical)	100 servers	5 days
Windows OS Vulnerability (8.0 – High)	200 servers	2 weeks
Tomcat EOL (10.0 – Critical)	20 systems	5 days
Adobe Professional Vulnerability (8.5 – High)	50 workstations	2 weeks
Google Chrome Vulnerabilities – multiple levels (8.7 – High)	50 workstations	2 weeks
Linux OS EOL (10.0 – Critical)	20 systems	5 days

Figure 5.3 Screenshot of what a report would look like.

The systems engineer is initially overwhelmed with the number of findings, which include Critical, High, Medium, and Low vulnerabilities. They are not quite sure where to start, what should be implemented first, and how to communicate these vulnerabilities with their team and management. After spending some time reviewing the report, they decide to start submitting items to the TRB for review. They also identify some controls which cannot be implemented at the time, based on customer requirements, and request exemptions back to the security team. But the systems engineer quickly becomes frustrated with the size of this file and the limited instructions provided by the security team. They do request a meeting with the assessor to determine how best to move forward with these findings.

From the assessor perspective, they are currently managing six different systems with six different teams, systems owners, management, and differing security requirements. The initial security assessment is due at the end of the week, and they must move on to the next security assessment. The assessor has spent weeks collecting information on the system, reviewing vulnerability reports, and consolidating the information into a spreadsheet. They do not have a background in IT operations, so they do not necessarily understand how the system operates. But they have reviewed the available system documentation to get a better understanding of how customers might interact with it. They are rushed at the end of the week with competing requirements, and send the report to the systems engineer, knowing that it may not be complete, but also providing an offer to explain findings or help to prioritize.

Even though the systems engineer responds and requests a meeting, they are already frustrated with the number of findings and lack of preliminary information. The assessor sets up the initial meeting, but they cannot meet for another week because they are starting a new project the next week.

The systems engineer becomes even more annoyed because now they have a week of waiting to find out how to address the findings. The engineer needs to start working on a new project to upgrade all their systems to the latest OS version, which will require a significant amount of their time and effort. Both the assessor and systems engineer need to move on to other projects that has been deemed by management as more important than the current assessment.

When the systems engineer and assessor meet after a week, the meeting is fraught with tension and misunderstanding. Both individuals are already frustrated when they arrive and find it difficult to come to an agreement on a path forward. The systems engineer argues that they will do the best they can given their new projects, and the assessor provides as much detail as possible for prioritizing the findings. The result is contention between both teams and lagging time for remediation and resolving the vulnerabilities identified in the initial report. All while new vulnerabilities, new patches, and additional security controls are found missing on the systems every day. This is a lose-lose situation and could have been handled much differently from the initial findings report.

IT VS CYBER: KO

This scenario will be taken from the viewpoint of a cybersecurity analyst who is working with a security assessor on remediating older findings. The analyst and security assessor are working through older exemptions on systems and have identified two older software vulnerabilities. These vulnerabilities are related to an EOL product on several servers throughout the environment. The exemption stated the software could not be updated because of customer requirements and constraints on the system. This exemption was supposed to expire 2 months prior, and the items should have been resolved. Upon inspecting updated vulnerability reports, the analyst and security assessor find that the software is still EOL and active on production servers.

After reviewing the findings, the analyst and security assessor schedule a meeting with the systems owner to discuss the exemption. Upon meeting, the systems owner becomes defensive and pinpoints that the system cannot be upgraded because it relies on the EOL software. The analyst and security assessor know that this is not true, that the system could be upgraded or migrated to new servers, but the process may be difficult. The systems owner notes that taking the system down, or rebuilding it, would potentially require downtime and would affect the revenue of the organization. The systems owner does not believe this is possible within the next year because it would be too much work on his small team.

The analyst and security assessor leave the meeting feeling frustrated and concerned over the lack of security on this system. They decide it is best to

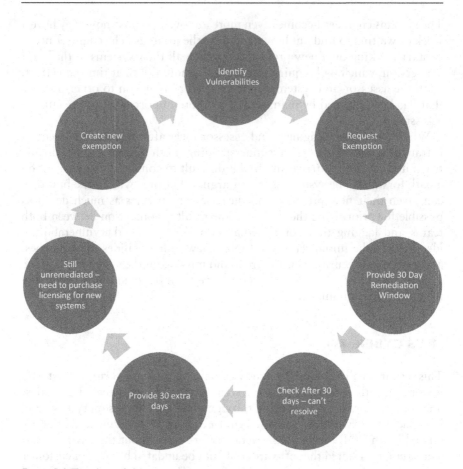

Figure 5.4 Timeline of the exemption.

work with management and notify them that the system is EOL and should be removed from the network. Security management and the CISO go back to the systems owner and their chain of command to address the finding. But the CIO and the IT management team push back on the upgrades because of the cost, potential downtime, loss of revenue, and difficulty of upgrading to new software. It would even require collaboration with a third party and partner to get this system fully upgraded and ready for the customer (Figure 5.4).

The management chain comes back and decides that six more months will be granted to allow time for upgrades. However, the analyst and security assessor see this as a failure of security for the system. The software was EOL a year prior, and the exemption is already 2 months overdue. They receive word back about the 6-month extension and are frustrated by the lack of concern over EOL software existing on customer-facing applications. They go back to their management teams and plead with them to move the timeline up for the overall security of the network. But the CIO and CISO have already agreed that 6 months will be an acceptable risk they are willing to take based on the nature of the vulnerabilities.

This situation may lead to a lack of trust from the analyst and security assessor perspective, regarding how management handled the situation. They would also feel frustrated that their concerns are not heard or validated by upper-level management. If this was the first instance of EOL software, or exemptions in general being waved, the cybersecurity team may brush it off and continue working. But after several instances of their concerns being ignored, they may consider leaving the organization to make a greater impact somewhere else. Situations like this lead to disgruntled employees, burnout, and eventually cybersecurity professionals leaving to find a better opportunity at another organization. This is a well-documented phenomenon within the cybersecurity industry.

EDUCATION

Education is a very hot topic between both IT and cybersecurity professions. There is a massive debate between how much education is required to perform tasks within IT or cybersecurity. Some IT and cybersecurity professionals feel that education is completely unnecessary, and even look down on individuals with higher levels of education. While others think that there is no possible why you can be successful in a technical field without a bachelor's degree in computer science. Like communication and differences in objectives, education is another area of contention and discord between IT and cybersecurity teams.

Historically, you did not need a computer science degree or software engineering degree to work on helpdesk or join an IT team as a junior administrator. A bachelor's degree may be helpful in acquiring a position, or even an internship while earning the degree, but was not seen as essential. And depending on the industry and size of the organization, they may still not require a bachelor's degree as an entry point into IT. Development roles may be a bit different, however, and a degree in software engineering from a trusted university would be vital in securing a role. There are many organizations and universities known for their programming and development degrees and are considered respected in the industry.

But there is still a stigma attached with higher education in IT. If an administrator or engineer earns a master's or graduate-level degree, they must want to become a lead or a manager. While there are some technical master's programs, several of them are aimed more at the management side of IT, infrastructure, networking, or telecommunications systems. An IT administrator may be immediately approached by management upon the completion of a graduate degree to determine if they are ready for a more senior or management role. However, a more technical Subject Matter Expert (SME) may not be as interested in a management position and prefer to stay hands-on.

A doctorate level degree in IT may be seen more suited for a CIO or Chief Technology Officer role, or even as an IT advisory role. A doctorate degree is also seriously frowned upon by a large part of the IT community. This level of education is seen as 'too academic' and as being too out of touch and away from the hands-on technical roles. While doctoral degrees for IT and IT management are more prevalent these days, it is still considered only appropriate for academic researchers, professors, or CIOs and board members for organizations. The level of stigma attached to doctoral degrees in IT leads to questions about someone being 'overqualified' for certain roles.

On the flip side, cybersecurity degrees and programs are being stood up at universities all over the world. This industry is experiencing such a boom that universities see the benefits of educating the next generation for cybersecurity roles. However, the same type of stigma is still attached to individuals who seek out a degree in cybersecurity versus receiving the hands-on training required for many roles. Some organizations may see a degree and no experience as a negative since the individual has not been in a real-world cybersecurity scenario. And even experienced cybersecurity professionals who have 10 years of experience may not have a degree because cybersecurity degrees are relatively new at institutions.

Whether IT or cybersecurity, there is contention within the teams and even discrimination against certain levels of education. There are some technical folks, on either side, that look down on people with bachelor's, master's, and doctorate degrees. This contention and negativity could lead to internal conflict, and then of course conflict between the two teams. Take for example an IT team that has received the level of bachelor's degrees, and they work with a team of cybersecurity professionals that have master's degrees and even a few doctoral degrees on the team. It is possible the IT team may be biased against the cybersecurity team based on their education and may not listen to their recommendations because they do not believe they are technical enough.

CERTIFICATIONS

Another hot topic within both IT and cybersecurity are certifications. The IT and cybersecurity education industries are huge money-making markets for organizations and institutions. As discussed in previous sections, certifications are available from a variety of groups and available in topics from digital forensics, incident response, OS levels, and vendor-specific applications. In both professions, certifications may be required for entry into the field, or if someone is looking to grow into a more senior role. For example, a Security+ certification from CompTIA could be required for a security analyst position, but an ISC2 CISSP certification would be required for a security engineer or architect position.

Within IT, there are more vendor-specific certifications available that may be required. For example, an IT administrator that manages an AD environment may need a Microsoft Azure AD certification. It could be a requirement from corporate or from a customer who wants to ensure that qualified staff are supporting them. Depending on job role, someone who manages an AWS deployment might need an AWS Cloud Practitioner certification, and a cloud architect might need the AWS Solutions Architect level certification. There is still some contention in the industry on what level of certifications are required, or if they are required at all.

But since the IT industry is expanding so quickly with new tools and types of technology, new certifications are being released constantly. Many vendors provide certifications on their products, so anyone could prove their expertise in products from (to name a few) Citrix, Microsoft, or AWS. Developers also have access to certifications in a variety of languages, and while not required for all roles, it does show expertise and experience. IT groups may still have disagreements between groups on what certifications are needed to perform the job role. The main issue with education and certifications is that most technical practitioners believe the best way to learn is to use the tools.

Cybersecurity is full of new certifications and while there are some vendor-specific security certifications, as in from AWS and Microsoft, there are many more vendor-agnostic certifications available. Organizations and universities provide domain-specific certifications instead, focusing on digital forensics, ethical hacking, risk management, and cloud security concepts. Certifications like ethical hacking or penetration testing may require hands-on skills labs or testing, but risk management or cybersecurity leadership may be multiple choice or scenario-based tests. Since many training providers are offering new training and certification courses, cybersecurity certifications are becoming another topic of debate. Are they really required to show expertise in cybersecurity, or a paperwork exercise that look good on resumes?

CONCLUSION

Whether education, certification, or role-based, discord exists between IT and cybersecurity teams. These groups may have differing opinions on what certifications (if any) are required to perform job roles, as well as what education level is appropriate. The problem with these differing opinions is that it may lead to a lack of trust or belief in someone's ability to provide technical instructions. For example, a cybersecurity engineer who happens to have ten separate certifications sends a report to an IT administrator.

The IT administrator sees the number of certifications in the signature line of the email which contains the report. Immediately their opinion changes of this cybersecurity engineer and they do not trust the report.

This could lead to lack of implementation of security controls, limited communication between the two groups, and ultimately poor security because of this perception of certifications. This is one scenario of how perception could affect security within an organization. Taking this one contact, this one moment in time, and multiple it by thousands or tens of thousands of interactions between IT and cybersecurity teams. Not every possible interaction could be covered here, but three examples of IT and cybersecurity meetings were explored. Each scenario shows how quickly mistrust, confusion, and frustration can occur between teams.

Ultimately, the ability to understand that a simple email could change someone's opinion is the first piece of this problem. The discord between teams could start with an email, a meeting, a bad day that translated to poor communication, or a variety of other interactions. Identifying how someone may perceive a situation can help determine why the situation ended up poorly and start working toward a resolution. But first it is just as important to understand the other factors that could lead to discord and frustration between IT and cybersecurity teams. This includes how separation of duties affects both groups, and how management interaction with the teams can change the conversation.

Chapter 6

Separation of duties

INTRODUCTION

Understanding why there may be contention between IT and cybersecurity teams is deeper than how the teams communicate and collaborate. There are many external security controls and risk management techniques that could be adding to miscommunication between teams. Separation of duties, job rotation, incident response (IR) activities, and the differences between daily tasking could all add tension. As well as how management on both sides interact with their own teams, as well as other groups within the organization.

To understand more comprehensively, it is important to dive into external factors that play into how teams operate inside and outside of their daily roles. For example, IT is required to create a policy to block certain websites by security teams, even though there are several that application owners will need access to. And even though the IT team may feel this is imposed by the security team, it may be from an IOC or finding related to an APT group. While the breadth of communication issues has been discussed, the depth and complexity of potential stressors will be explored more in this section.

SEPARATION OF DUTIES

Separation of duties is a common concept throughout IT and cybersecurity and has been a component of security assessments and audits for many years. The idea is that a system owner would not be responsible for the management and operations of a system, as well as the vulnerability scanning and remediation. This ensures that the individual managing the system is not missing vulnerabilities or saying that items are fixed when the controls are not. This also provides an extra check for the IT administrators from the security side to verify settings are properly in place. The National Institute of Standards and Technology (NIST) defines separation of duties as the 'principle that no user should be given enough privileges to misuse the system on their own' (Hu et al., 2017).

Another good example of separation of duties is that an IT administrator would not have access to every single system within the environment. An

DOI: 10.1201/9781003264422-6

administrator who manages the email system may not have permissions to the encryption or Public Key Infrastructure (PKI) system. This ensures that if an employee becomes disgruntled or frustrated, they could only make changes to a subset of systems and hopefully not take down the entire network. And in a similar way, with limited permissions on systems, administrators would not be able to make changes that would affect another area of the environment. If an attacker was able to compromise an administrator account, if they only had access to certain systems, it may take them longer to compromise multiple systems.

Separation of duties between IT and cybersecurity teams are typically in place to help improve the security and validity of controls which are put in place. Based on the NIST Risk Management Framework (RMF), IT administrators would typically choose and implement the technical controls, while the security teams would assess and monitor them to verify that they are still in place. This separation of duties ensures that the same IT administrator who implements the controls is not responsible for reporting that those controls are still in place over time. And this is not necessarily to say that an IT administrator would do something malicious; it provides a failsafe and extra set of verification for security controls (Figure 6.1).

But sometimes separation of duties means that the same IT administrator who runs multiple OS and applications, is unable to scan their own

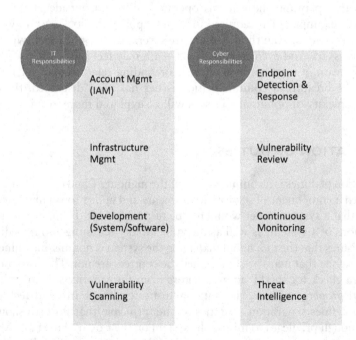

Figure 6.1 Separation of duties.

machines for vulnerabilities. Meaning that these administrators would have to contact the security team any time they wanted to run vulnerability or configuration scans to verify that vulnerabilities were remediated. A request may be made via email or a ticketing system, which could add on to time between the request and the time of scan and associated report. It could be another contributing factor to frustration or increased stress levels for needing an intermediary to run vulnerability scans.

On the other side, cybersecurity teams more than likely do not have administrator access to systems. This means they cannot make changes, review local settings on servers, or even review policies in management consoles without proper access. If a security analyst knows of a vulnerability and the IT administrator is unsure of how to make the change, the analyst would have to provide written instructions for remediation. For example, there is a registry key that needs to be applied via a group policy and the setting should be at '0'. The IT administrator puts in the group policy, but the setting is at '1', which does not remediate the finding. If the analyst had the proper AD experience and was able to change the setting, it would save a lot of 'back and forth' communication.

Cybersecurity analysts and engineers who have a background in IT operations or administration may have the proper skillset to implement controls. But this would not align with separation of duties, and if a change is made without the knowledge or consent of the system owner, functionality or operational issues could occur. And if the changes are made to align with security, but do not meet the availability concerns, both IT and security teams may disagree on a proper solution. There are many scenarios where separation of duties may inhibit or change the decisions made throughout IT and cybersecurity teams.

JOB ROTATION

Job rotation is another typical control put in place to ensure that individuals are moved through different roles to reduce burnout, train in a variety of roles in case a team member is on vacation, and to make sure that multiple people can perform the same role. This control is put in place to ensure that, specifically in helpdesk and Security Operations Center (SOC) teams, that individuals do not burn out and leave the organization. Helpdesk teams and SOCs can be very stressful environments, and without job rotation or the ability to move up in their career, technicians and analysts may move on quickly to other roles. The NIST National Initiative for Cybersecurity Education framework mentions rotating staff into different positions to develop new skills (NISTb, 2017) (Figure 6.2).

Job rotation has other benefits, where an individual may be trained by a security engineer on a specific tool, when the security engineer moves to a senior role, their junior can take over management of the system. It provides an opportunity to keep someone in a backfill position, while also upskilling

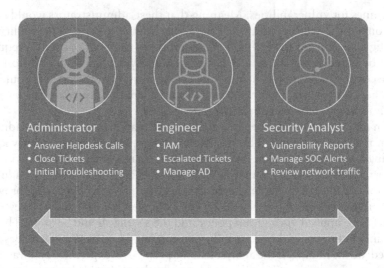

Figure 6.2 Diagram of job rotation duties.

new and junior employees. This keeps a constant rotation of new employees to push into more senior roles and allow for more flexibility for individuals to try other types of roles within their own organization. However, job rotation may not be a formal process or something that is well defined in HR policies. It could be a more informal opportunity that the management offers to their team members to learn new skills, try a different type of job, or allow them to grow in their own position.

But while this is mentioned in several older NIST guides, there is not a lot of updated information on this practice. Job rotation can help to not only improve security practices, but also cut down on employee fraud and abuse, specifically in the finance sector. But job rotation can also be a catalyst for improving relationships between IT and cybersecurity teams. Consider an organization that details IT administrators for 6 weeks to the SOC to learn about alerts and continuous monitoring. Or, on the other side, consider a security assessor who works with the cloud engineering team for 6 weeks to learn about standard operations.

TYPICAL IT DUTIES

To continue the discussion of separation of duties and job rotations, IT roles and daily tasks will be discussed in brief. Most newer IT functions are based on the management and operations of cloud systems, infrastructure, managing mobile devices, IAM policy and management, as well as communication methods and encryption. This is not an exhaustive list, and it is more possible to find IT specialists who manage a specific vendor product, or suite of products. For example, an IT administrator may manage the Microsoft Office 365 deployment and operations as their main job function. Or a cloud administrator may manage a subset of systems within the cloud infrastructure, including policies, IAM, server OS templates, and terraform scripts. But the cloud administrator would not have access to the Office 365 management console, and the IT administrator would not have access to the cloud infrastructure with administrative permissions.

A day for an IT administrator may include starting with emails from management and teammates, checking trouble tickets, patching, or updating systems, and meeting with other teams on functionality concerns. They may or may not interact with security daily, if they are not close with the team, they may only see them once a month for audits or security reviews. They might receive daily or weekly vulnerability reports, so within a week, change tickets would be submitted to remediate findings or apply patches. For the IT administrator managing Office 365, they may work on tickets related to user complaints, installing patches, changing security group members, or updating policies to align with corporate guidance.

The point is that anyone handling IT or OT (Operational Technology) functions will be immersed in the functionality and operability of the products they configure and manage. Security may be a second thought because of the immense pressure for systems to be available and operational for users. They may even have a Service Level Agreement that requires uptime of 99% for all products, meaning that if they have an outage, the operations team must address it quickly. There must also be HA functionality built in, and constant review of how the systems would handle an outage using Disaster Recovery (DR) planning. It is possible to have overlap between DR and IR activities, but DR would typically be tested by IT, and IR concerns are handled by security teams.

Regarding vulnerability scans and reports, IT administrators may only receive basic information to conduct remediation activities. They may be provided a report, a list of vulnerabilities, a screenshot of the vulnerability details, or an email with the findings. Another method might be the findings after an audit or security assessment, which could be a rather lengthy document. It may also not provide a good path forward for remediation, the information could be vague or map to a security control without context. This can make it difficult for the IT administrator to make the required changes, and thus a never-ending back and forth between IT and cybersecurity teams begins.

TYPICAL CYBER DUTIES

In a similar way, a cybersecurity analyst would start the day with emails from systems owners and maybe security assessors/auditors, meeting about security assessments or engineering projects, and managing security tools. But in contrast to IT teams, cybersecurity teams are constantly reviewing open-source information for latest types of attacks, newest vulnerabilities, zero-day exploits, and how to remediate newer styles of attacks. IT groups may be reviewing new tools and technologies, but not necessarily the latest in cyberattacks. Or at least, from the IT perspective it is more about inspecting what may impact their systems, not what would impact the organization.

An IT administrator may be concerned with the users or how well their system is functioning, and a security analyst is more concerned with how many instances of a zero-day vulnerability exist within the environment. The security analyst would be using the open-source information to conduct threat hunting operations, scanning the environment for IOCs like known malicious IPs, file hashes, or file names of malware or malicious executables. While there may be some other policy updates or management for security tools, focus is primarily on identifying concerns in systems and working to have them resolved quickly.

Cybersecurity analysts and engineers may also be proactively scanning the environment to find security gaps that are not found in vulnerability scans. For example, a vulnerability scan may show missing patches or misconfigured security controls but may not show that Multi-Factor Authentication is missing on an application management console for administrators. These types of findings usually require additional research, communication between systems owners and IT administrators, and technical evidence to determine if the finding is legitimate. One finding on the cybersecurity side could mean weeks of meetings, emails, and research to simply identify that it does exist. If that could lead to change of management processes like TRB boards that would need to approve the change, then it would be scheduled by the systems owners.

These types of situations can be frustrating for cybersecurity analysts when it spends weeks or months to remediate one finding on one system. It could be even more concerning if the finding becomes an exemption for 6 months, or even becomes a waiver of the control and the risk is accepted for the organization. All the research, meetings, and writing reports for one finding to have it be waived and not remediated. And this frustration could be compounded when they receive pushback in emails from systems owners or administrators who do not think the finding is significant.

INCIDENT RESPONSE

IR is a classic scenario where separation of duties can be a distractor or may encumber the situation. IT and cybersecurity groups have separate responsibilities when it comes to IR activities. IR is when an incident, or potential incident, is identified during typical business operations. The incident could be a malware download, a malicious word document downloaded from an email, or network traffic that is connecting with known bad IPs. IR would be a set of policies, guidelines, tools, and techniques used by an organization to respond to different types of attacks or incidents. Incidents could be from a malicious outside attacker, or from a disgruntled employee who is attempting to exfiltrate data.

An IR policy would dictate the roles and responsibilities of anyone involved in an incident. For example, it would outline who to contact in the event of an incident, appropriate communication channels, and responsibilities of systems owners and cybersecurity analysts. A cybersecurity analyst may collect initial information, contain infected machines, or review network traffic to identify patterns, whereas the system owner may be responsible for contacting upper-level management, notifying customers of impact, and writing up a report of the initial incident. In the event of a ransomware attack, for instance, a group of advisors may be called to review the information before determining whether to contact law enforcement or pay the fine.

Responsibilities in an incident are clearly defined, and based on the level of permissions, IT and cybersecurity teams involved may not have access to all relevant information. Handling an incident quickly and containing threats entails a high level of effective communication. But separation of duties may mean waiting for screenshots, technical settings, or on-demand vulnerability scans for updated information. This could mean more time to identify and ultimately remediate any zero-day exploits. And anyone in cybersecurity knows that the time to remediate findings is critical when it is actively being exploited in the wild.

Consider a scenario like the SolarWinds situation in 2020. When the information was released publicly about which products were affected, cybersecurity teams distributed the information as quickly as possible to management and as many contacts as possible. Cybersecurity groups were scrambling to identify the vulnerable products, who were the systems owners, and coordinating remediation. And IT administrators were working just as quickly to identify which versions and which products were currently being used, and what impact it would have on the environment if systems were turned off. IT teams were working to keep the systems online because without them, they lost a lot of their operations capabilities and ability to see server health.

PERMISSIONS

Permissions are another layer of complexity to the separation of duties conundrum. Permissions are what level of access someone has to data, systems, or consoles. Access may be role-based, meaning availability of data would be based on the type of employee. Level of access might also be based

Figure 6.3 Example table of IT and cyber permissions.

on rules, so when someone logs in during business hours they have access to certain files, but after 5 pm access would be turned off. Both styles of access could be used within an organization to create a complex structure of permissions (Figure 6.3).

In the context of IT and cybersecurity teams, permissions could inhibit access to pertinent information or limit ability to review vulnerability reports. IT administrators would most likely not have administrative access to vulnerability scanners or the antivirus or anti-malware solutions. However, if IT manages the antivirus solutions and the cybersecurity team is not able to alter configurations or review alerts, it could cause contention between teams. If there is an alert found in the antivirus console, and the security team is not notified immediately, it could possibly lead to full system compromise. That is a worst-case scenario, but still a possible outcome if cybersecurity teams are missing permissions to see malicious alerts.

For cybersecurity teams, they more often do not have administrative views into applications, cloud deployments, or OS configuration. They view servers and applications through the window of how many vulnerabilities or missing security controls they have. It may be difficult for a security analyst to understand all the settings that co-exist and work together within a system, if they do not have a background in IT. Without even view permissions to OS or application consoles, they may have a difficult time seeing how changing those controls would affect a system. For example, the cybersecurity team recommends turning off SolarWinds servers to mitigate a zero-day vulnerability until they can investigate for potential system compromise (or stop further compromise from occurring). The cybersecurity team would not necessarily know how much it would impact daily IT operations tasks if those servers were shut down.

The inability to view, change, or even test settings because of limited permission can inhibit progress during incidents. This situation could also lead to mistrust, if the IT group says that they have turned off all vulnerable systems, but the cybersecurity team finds more vulnerable systems after a fresh scan. The cybersecurity team would not trust future information from the IT team, and the IT team may feel frustrated that there was a system on the network they were not aware of, and therefore did not identify initially. Permissions (or lack of permissions) could lead to increased time to identify problems, mistrust between teams, and inability to effectively complete job tasks.

SILOED TEAMS

With the need for separation of duties, IT and cybersecurity teams may be scattered and fractured through the organization. Even within IT, cloud engineers, operations groups, IAM, and specialized product teams could have little contact with each other. These teams may get together when there is a functionality issue, an outage, or on a new project that requires multiple skillsets. But daily or even weekly interaction between teams may not be required, and since everyone in an IT group is already overloaded with work, they might limit interaction with other teams. It is possible that through multiple years working together on projects or outages, they would have friendly interactions and be aware of each other.

But IT and cybersecurity teams may not have the same type of interactions and communication. Cybersecurity teams are so focused on alerts, research, and investigations and not on the operations or outages that IT groups may experience. Cybersecurity groups would most likely not have daily interaction with the IT team except when dealing with an incident or zero-day exploit. These groups may be siloed, meaning that they do not interact or communicate in any kind of consistent manner. It is possible that the lack of interaction is simply because the teams do not know each other. If they sit on different floors, or if the organization is large enough, they may not even know of all the other teams within the company.

But if IT and cybersecurity teams have zero interaction, or they only know of each other through tickets and emails, how well can they work together? Without understanding each teams' objectives, goals, daily tasks, and even what kind of personalities they have, can they have effective communication? To break it down to a very human perspective, if an IT administrator does not know a cybersecurity analyst personally, what do they think of them and how would that affect their interactions? In prior sections, the ideas of *people*, *process*, and *technology* were discussed in broad terms. But the *people* aspect of this concept highly affects siloed teams.

For example, an IT group that only hears from the cybersecurity analysts in the SOC when there is an alert or machine that needs to be contained. Their only interaction is negative in the sense that it is another incident or possible incident that inhibits daily tasks and project work. Meaning that the exchanges are typically negative and could require them to work extra hours or detract from what they need to accomplish that day. If IT and cybersecurity groups only interact during a poor security assessment, a failed audit, or to provide a listing of vulnerabilities, how can these groups see each other in a positive way?

HELPING OR HURTING?

Siloed teams, limited permissions for tools, IR activities, and separation of duties are all contributing factors to how IT and cybersecurity teams interact. Job rotation and separation of duties are typical security controls and would be addressed on most security audits. IR programs could be well documented or may be less mature without any process or procedures in place. Limited permissions, as a construct of separation of duties, could impact both abilities to perform tasks as well as quick resolution of vulnerabilities. Each aspect of separation of duties could positively or negatively impact the effectiveness of the cybersecurity program.

On the positive side, including separation of duties meets several security control requirements included in an audit. Separation of duties may be an unavoidable control, regardless of impact on the teams. However, separating IT and cybersecurity duties may also help with burnout and overworked staff. If an IT administrator was responsible for the management, configuration, patching, and vulnerability scanning and reporting for all systems, it may be too much to manage. The ability to split tasks also provides an additional layer of confirmation that security settings are in place and are verified by two different groups. There are a few positive aspects to separation of duties and keeping groups somewhat siloed.

However, there are far more concerns with separation of duties and having teams that are siloed. Without open lines of communication between the individual's managing the systems and those trying to secure them, how effective are the security controls? Not knowing who is on the other end of an email requesting remediation of vulnerabilities, there may also be mistrust or confusion which leads to further contention. The lack of visibility from cybersecurity teams to the general population of users means that users do not have any clue as to what the group does. Mistrust is one of the security controls that is a by-product of siloed teams.

Another major concern for separation of duties is the conversation about how much permissions are appropriate for job roles. There is no one right answer for this problem since every organization will have different sized IT and cybersecurity teams. Typically, if cybersecurity groups cannot make changes on systems, and the IT administrator does not know how to make the change, this increases time between vulnerability identification to remediation. Troubleshooting requires emails, video calls or in-person meetings, and time spent explaining the issue back and forth before it can be resolved. Additional time would be required to re-scan the systems and verify the setting was in place, which includes continuous monitoring to make sure the setting did not get removed accidently over time.

Finally, a major concern of separation of duties is the impact that it has on the time spent on vulnerabilities. As mentioned previously, time from identification to resolving a vulnerability is critical. Within the span that a vulnerability is analyzed and submitted into the Common Vulnerabilities and Exposures index, to the time that it is identified in an environment, it could be exploited in the wild. All the additional emails, meetings, and confusion on a vulnerability could lead to account compromise, ransomware attacks,

Distributed Denial of Service (DDoS) attacks, or (worst-case scenario) full system compromise. If cybersecurity groups could be given temporary permissions and have more consistent contact with IT teams, vulnerabilities may be resolved more quickly and increase trust between groups.

CONCLUSION

The functionality and security of a system is not dependent solely on technical implementations, assessments, and frameworks. The challenges of creating a secure environment are complex and layered within how teams operate and communicate. Even reviewing the differences between IT and cybersecurity teams regarding daily tasking show how quickly teams may miscommunicate or misunderstand each other. If an IT administrator is concerned about making a policy change because a similar setting took down the system before, a cybersecurity analyst has a choice on how to handle the situation. They could immediately go to management, write up a report based on their concerns, ignore the finding, or work on options with the administrator.

It is essential for IT and cybersecurity teams to consider the frameworks and guidance that currently exist in their organizations. Does separation of duties exist in policy only, or as a mechanism built into the products and technology in the environment? Consider how separation of duties and other aspects of common security functions exist within IT teams, and between IT and security teams. Are siloed teams inside the IT or security teams, as well within the groups? In larger organizations IT or development teams may be separate and have little contact based on their job functions or the products they support.

REFERENCES

Hu, V. C., Kuhn, R., & Yaga, D. (2017). SP 800-192: Verification and test methods for access control policies/models. doi:106028/NIST.SP.800-192.
NIST (2017). National initiative for cybersecurity education (NICE) cybersecurity workforce. doi:10.6028/NIST.SP.800-181.

Chapter 7

Management interaction

MANAGEMENT INTERACTION

Managers for IT and cybersecurity provide guidance, prioritization of tasking and projects, as well as coordination between teams to have changes approved or procure budgeting for resources. Management can also be a trusted advisor in the technical space when their background is in operations, security, development, or engineering. Working with analysts and engineers, managers must understand the daily operations and ongoing projects to be an effective leader. They can help to provide prioritization for tasking when a team is feeling overwhelmed or overloaded with multiple projects at once. They can also be an effective middle-point between executive leadership and technical staff when dealing with outages or delays in product deployments.

For projects that require coordination between IT and cybersecurity management groups, like the way that an IT administrator and security analyst would work together, communication is an important tool. Without effective communication, technical projects may fail, disharmony could erupt between teams, and ultimately the environment could be insecure. For example, executive management recently requested the office to move from an on-premises email solution to Office 365. Without the integration of the security team from the onset of the project, IT management may be held responsible for any delays based on security assessments or identified vulnerabilities. But if IT and cybersecurity management collaborate early in the project, that could alleviate potential interruptions in the schedule.

IT and cybersecurity management have differing skillsets, concerns, and priorities in an organization. IT management are focused on project management, operations, functionality of systems, and aligning with executive and business strategy. On the IT side, there may also be a need to fulfill customer requirements and keep customer-facing systems running based on Service Level Agreements (SLAs). Whereas cybersecurity management are concerned with risks to systems, vulnerabilities and zero-day exploits, and how to handle an incident. On the cybersecurity side, management would also be focused on security policy, associated business regulations, and how to prioritize risk management activities. A common goal between both groups

DOI: 10.1201/9781003264422-7

is to align with the business strategy, and this is a critical component for the success or failure of either team.

To identify where discord may exist between IT and cybersecurity groups, relationships between engineers, analysts, team leads, and management will be explored in depth. Each relationship, whether vertical or horizontal in the organization, could positively or negatively impact daily operations. For example, something as simple as bringing donuts to a meeting could represent a 'peace offering' and improve the moods of attendees. Especially if management is bringing bad news to higher ups or sharing potential issues with projects. On the other side, if a manager brings an operations issue to executives because someone made a mistake several hours after the incident occurred, this could lead to mistrust and anger. Whereas if the issue had been brought to executives early on in detection and a clear plan was provided, executives may be more understanding.

SOC LEADS

Security Operations Center (SOC) leads, and really anyone in an operations environment, work in a stressful environment. There is a constant barrage of alerts, threats, and vulnerabilities that need to be reviewed and assessed quickly. Without quick identification of a possible threat to the network, account or full system compromise could occur. SOC leads know this concern intimately, as most of them have lived through at least one incident in their career. Typically, they have several years of experience in an SOC, and may have an IT operations background as well. They are responsible for identification of possible incidents, communication of each level of threat, and managing how the SOC is run. Depending on the style of the team, they may run 24/7 and through holidays, which means they are very susceptible to burnout (Figure 7.1).

Any SOC lead also knows the inherent risks of the job, including the high turnover rate of SOC analysts. They are also very aware that blame could fall

SOC Responsibilities
Monitoring Alerts

Review EDR Console

Respond to Tickets

Review Vulnerabilities

Create Documentation

Investigate Possible Incidents

Respond to Incident Activities

Figure 7.1 SOC responsibilities.

on them for an incident, even if it was handled well and contained quickly. In most operations groups, IT or cybersecurity, there is a running joke that being fired is part of the job. And while not a particularly funny joke, it is a reality that SOC leads could be blamed for any incident and be held responsible for whatever fallout occurs (data breach, ransomware event, etc.). And in combination with keeping up with any active alerts, cases, or potential incidents, they must also be aware of any current threats to the organization and active zero-day exploits in the wild.

But SOC leads must also be able to communicate quickly and concisely to upper levels of management. They require superior decision-making skills to understand what information needs to go to what level of management. For example, if malware was found and contained on a machine with limited impact on the network, that may not be a reportable incident. But if a ransomware package was dropped on a few devices (but not executive), and even if the malicious packages were spotted early and removed quickly, this would still be considered an incident in many organizations. This is because if someone is targeting the organization with a ransomware attack, they will most likely try again or continue at the very least scanning their networks combing for vulnerabilities.

SOC leads must also collaborate with their IT operations counterparts because a cybersecurity attack can quickly affect the functionality of systems. If machines must be contained due to malware or malicious files detected, the IT group may need to be notified so that the helpdesk does not get inundated with calls and emails. If the helpdesk is unaware that machines were contained, they may spend hours trying to fix and issue that they did not have visibility to. This one situation is another example of how lack of permissions or visibility to other areas of the business can inhibit troubleshooting efforts. SOC leads must be the intermediaries between other teams and raise the alarms to the right people at the right time.

IT OPERATIONS LEADS

In a similar way to their SOC lead counterparts, IT operations leads are under a lot of pressure to keep systems running for either internal or external customers. One of the things a general user may not consider or be aware of, operations groups consider all users as customers. In that way, IT operations leads ensure the alignment of projects, engineering, and operations tasks that impact their system or subset of systems within the organization. In a smaller organization, there may be one IT operations lead for the entire network, whereas in a larger organization an IT operations lead may have 10–20 team members and manage one specific product. In the larger organization, an example would be managing the cloud infrastructure, but not the email, mobile device management, specialty applications, or encryption technologies.

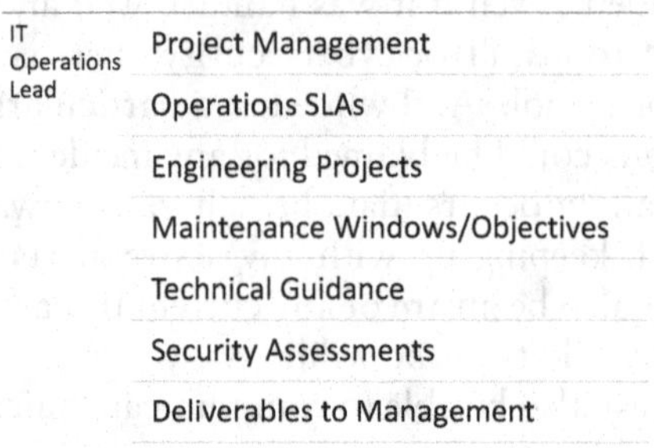

IT Operations Lead	Project Management
	Operations SLAs
	Engineering Projects
	Maintenance Windows/Objectives
	Technical Guidance
	Security Assessments
	Deliverables to Management

Figure 7.2 IT ops leads tasking diagram.

IT operations leads more than likely come with a background in some sort of operations group, whether helpdesk or managing a customer-facing solution. For example, they may have come from a team where they deploy virtual desktops and applications for users. With this experience comes years of handling user tickets and complex problems, outages, and long nights troubleshooting or applying patches. They may have to follow certain maintenance windows to resolve issues or remediate vulnerabilities, for example 4:00–6:00 am on Friday mornings. This time would be dedicated to the operations groups and is a notification to users that they may experience interruptions during that time (Figure 7.2).

More often, IT operations leads have the technical operations or engineering experience and may have some college education and technical certifications. They would still be hands-on with systems and still manage high-level changes or step in to solve complicated problems. IT operations leads are trusted advisors for team members when questions arise around priority of tasking. For example, if a network engineer needs to perform system upgrades, solve five trouble tickets related to separate VLANs, and resolve two vulnerabilities. The engineer may go to the team lead to help determine which issue is most pressing and should be resolved first. And if problems arise during the maintenance window with upgrades, the team lead would step in to provide technical guidance and communicate issues up to management.

And like their cybersecurity counterparts, IT operations leads are familiar with the stress that comes in an operations environment. Juggling multiple projects, scheduling upgrades within maintenance windows, working with vendors on troubleshooting calls, are all part of a typical day. They must also coordinate with security analysts, engineers, or auditors when vulnerabilities are identified. They juggle the security concerns and customer requirements to align with what is best for the business and ultimately what management has determined is most important. IT operations leads would provide their technical advice and expertise to team members as well as to upper-level management.

SECURITY MANAGEMENT

A Security Manager (SM), depending on the size of the organization, would oversee one large security group, or possibly several smaller security groups. In a larger setting, SMs would manage the SOC, a security engineering team, a threat intelligence team, the insider threat group, or an incident response team. But in a smaller organization the SM might manage all these disciplines within the organization. With a smaller team, an SM would have very different responsibilities versus a larger business with an increased budget and more available resources. An SM provides oversight for all security objectives in the organization and is either also the Chief Information Security Officer (CISO) or reports directly to the CISO.

An SM would have extensive experience in the IT or cybersecurity field, whether in operations, engineering, development or within an SOC or IR team. A cybersecurity manager's skillset would range quite a bit since the cybersecurity field contains so many domains. Like an IT specialist and generalist, cybersecurity managers could be a specialist in vulnerability management or insider threat but would complement the specialty with a breadth of industry knowledge. The most important skill for an SM is to understand challenges across a cybersecurity program and understand how disparate teams need to work together on complex problems. The further up in an organization that a cybersecurity manager works, the more business strategy alignment becomes important in problem-solving (Figure 7.3).

A cybersecurity manager would need to collaborate with executive management, whether a CISO or Chief Information Officer (CIO), as well as IT and cybersecurity team leads, product owners, and other groups within the organization. In the event of an incident, they will provide updates and coordinate between executives and the operations teams who are performing the work. One major skill of an SM is the ability to create concise and accurate information to help inform executives. They must also have the technical expertise to understand a situation and be able to translate that for executive management. In the time of an incident or data breach, SMs act as a communication throughput to ingest technical information and output it in a concise and higher-level format.

Without a technical background, an SM may have some difficulty understanding the depth of a problem and misinterpret the findings. For example, if there is a zero-day vulnerability announced that is being exploited in the wild, an SM may be receiving reports from the SOC. They received a report on a possible exploit taking place actively on a system, and the SOC wants to know if they should contain those systems or turn them off completely. If the SM does not have the technical expertise to understand how the exploit operates and could affect the environment, they may not be able to provide the most accurate advice. However, in that case, hopefully they have team leads who can help them make that decision.

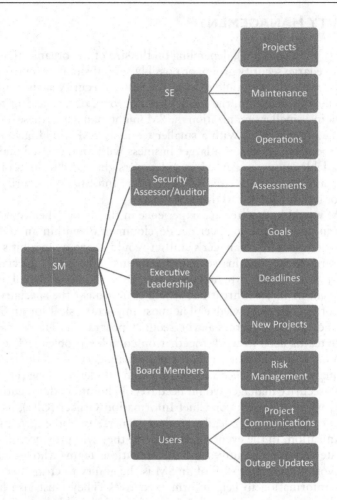

Figure 7.3 ISSM communication chain.

In the case of a poor security assessment on a group of systems in the environment, the SM may be responsible for helping to coordinate remediation activities. IT management may also come to the SM for guidance on what can be waived, exempted, or is considered a mitigating control. Without collaboration and offering to assist, tension could arise between the IT and cybersecurity teams. There could also be tension caused by the lack of coordination between IT and security management structures, which trickles down to the operations teams. If management does not communicate well with each other, how could they communicate well with their own teams? Discord between teams is horizontal and vertical both up and down throughout management chains.

IT MANAGEMENT

IT management, like cybersecurity managers, may come from a technical team where they managed one or several products. However, IT managers could also have a background in project management and move into IT. It is not a realistic expectation that all IT management have a background in operations and engineering; however, that can add to the confusion between teams. Individuals who move into higher-level IT management roles may come from a variety of backgrounds, and in fairness, bring skills from other sectors and types of roles. They may manage one product or service offering, or in smaller organizations they may manage the entire IT infrastructure under the leadership of the CIO.

The main functions of an IT manager include working with executive management and the technical team leads to help ensure functionality and operability. If there is an outage, they would help to manage communications between executives and potentially customers. More than likely, they would be approving communications to users or customers, and providing executive management with frequent updates. If an outage took multiple days, they would be responsible for bringing the systems back online, as well as working on an After-Action Report. The After-Action Report would provide details on what happened, who was involved, how the issue was resolved, and what technical review will be conducted to ensure it does not happen again.

IT management would also help to guide projects and work with security teams on assessments and audits. This is a more high-level position that would be engaged more if there are issues or coordination needs to occur between teams. An IT manager would not necessarily be 'hands-on keyboard' but would provide technical guidance and offer solutions when a team is stuck on a project. With a larger team, a manager may work more with team leads, and with a smaller team they may be more involved in the tools and technology and working with administrators and engineers. When it comes to working on multiple projects, they must multi-task and communicate across the organization.

Working with security teams and with the CIO on security concerns would be another task on an IT manager's plate. They must balance the need for operations and customer requirements, as well as any lingering exemptions or security concerns. In the case of a security incident, an IT manager would be heavily involved in the coordination of remediation or mitigation. They would be collaborating frequently between engineers, leads, executives, and working on updated communications. They may also be coordinating reports between IT and security to determine what the risk level is in the environment. Any security incidents, audits, or security assessment results would be a factor into how projects would proceed or need to be updated to align with the findings (Figure 7.4).

An IT manager could be the difference between success and failure of IT objectives. A well-run IT shop that allows engineers and administrators to

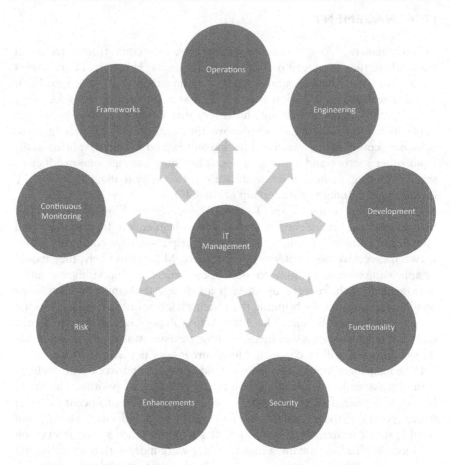

Figure 7.4 Path to IT management.

thrive, will lead to successful projects and positive interactions. But an IT manager that is not interested in security objectives or has had poor interactions with a security group could lead to the lack of security controls or delayed implementation. When IT and security managers communicate often, especially if there is a concern or incident, remediation can be done quickly and painlessly. If there is a lack of coordination there could be confusion, for example, if there was a network vulnerability, that was actively exploited in the wild. If the security team expressed urgency for patching, based on the active exploitation, and the IT management was not concerned and did not notify the team right away. It is possible those devices would be compromised before they could be patched, potentially leading to a cybersecurity incident with loss of data or fully compromised systems.

CISO ENGAGEMENT

Anyone in a CISO role is aware of the immense pressure on them to create a secure environment and provide a quick response time for incidents. CISO's primary function is to understand and provide guidance for risk management across the organization. They may come from a management or technical background, but would be very aware of security threats, new vulnerabilities, as well as the possible implications from industry guidance. The CISO role is an excellent place for someone with cybersecurity industry knowledge, impeccable communication and organizational skills, as well as the ability to problem solve quickly. While the CISO role is relatively new for many organizations, it has become an important role to support risk management and cybersecurity objectives.

But there is quite a bit of debate on where a CISO should report, whether to the CEO, the CIO, or straight to the Board of Directors. In most organizations, the CISO reports to the CIO, although the thought behind that reporting structure is starting to change. A CISO is responsible for all cybersecurity initiatives within the organization, but ultimately, some security tools and alerting may fall under the CIO's purview. Antivirus, network security, and Endpoint Detection and Response (EDR) may still fall under the CIO and IT operations groups. But the impact and analysis from those tools may be needed for review by the SOC or the security analysts under the CIO. This can create confusion on the management and operations of security tools, especially if the security analysts and engineers are unable to review alerts or configuration of the tools.

The CISO may be responsible for some security assets, but also would be responsible for the creation and management of company-wide security policy, guidance, and adherence to security standards. If there is a Chief Technology Officer (CTO), the CISO may report to the CIO along with the CTO. Hopefully, there is collaboration between all three parties, but the more executives that work in a larger organization may have immense pressure on the amount of assets and responsibilities they have. When balancing functionality, operations, effectiveness, and security objectives, executives would fight for their teams and budgets. If teams are stretched for budget or resources, and their respective executives need to fight against other groups for an increased budget, this can also lead to discord.

Cybersecurity teams, classically, have smaller budgets than IT or development teams. Considering that cybersecurity teams may not even manage all the associated security tool, the budget may be more strained than their IT counterparts. Since cybersecurity teams are typically small and need to be agile, the CISO may be taking on additional duties and responsibilities to help the team. Of course, budgets and team sizes vary wildly, and this is just an example of how a team would operate. But there is a lot of evidence and research that point to security teams being smaller and requiring more ingenuity or fewer employees doing more work. And with smaller teams, increased workloads, and smaller budgets comes quick burnout and frustration of the employees on the team.

In larger environments, a CISO would have more flexibility to acquire the tools they want, hire the SMEs and analysts they need, and respond quickly to incidents. One thing all CISOs have in common though is the need to secure their environments with whatever they have at their disposal, and in most cases, the ability to adapt quickly and understand the current challenges within their cybersecurity program. But to make the most of their budgets and available resources, a positive collaboration with the CIO can go a long way to improve the overall security on a network. Without a positive collaboration, and the ability to communicate risks to the CIO and CEO, cybersecurity teams would remain small and security objectives would not be raised to higher levels.

CIO ENGAGEMENT

CIOs have immense responsibility at organizations, even more so in the last 10 years than any time prior. With the advancements in software development, increased development projects within organizations, as well as the increased risk management concerns, CIOs are taking on more than ever before. In larger organizations with software development projects, there is more than likely a Chief Product Officer or an executive running the software engineering objectives. However, this does not mean that the CIO is not supportive or in collaboration with the Chief Product Officer to provide infrastructure or the management of specialty applications to support the engineers. The CIO would report to the CEO, but may have other executives like the CISO, reporting directly to them.

A CIO more than likely has a heavy management background with a focus or specialty in some technology. Whether an IT specialist or generalist, a CIO possesses some serious technical and management skills to orchestrate a successful IT infrastructure. With technology moving at an insanely fast pace, CIOs must run their organization with agility and efficiency. They must balance functionality, security, operations, business strategy, customer and user objectives, along with regulatory requirements. CIOs manage the policy, IT strategy, and have the foresight to plan the next 5–10 years of IT development. Juggling the people, process, and technology goals for the entire organization, CIOs collaborate with many teams and must understand their unique requirements.

In a considerable number of environments, the CISO reports to the CIO. There is much debate on where the CISO should sit, but it is important to break down what this standard relationship looks like. A CIO does not necessarily have experience or a background in cybersecurity, nor do they always consider it a main concern. This is not a knock at CIOs, and this is another example of how objectives and priorities shift based on type of role and alignment with the business strategy. Each role supports their own unique teams and goals, and in the case of the CIO, business alignment and support of users are most important. When working with a CISO, the CIO would regard them as an expert in cybersecurity and expect them to prioritize any risks and concerns, notify them of any incidents, and potential security concerns within IT projects and systems.

With a positive relationship between a CIO and a CISO, both technology and cybersecurity goals can be met with an appropriate strategy and balance between teams. If a CIO understands and appreciates cybersecurity objectives in alignment with the business, there would be few issues. However, if a CIO does not trust the information from a CISO or is not as concerned with the cybersecurity program, a CISO organization may be short-staffed and underfunded. This also means that the overall risk management program within the organization would suffer from lack of communication, misunderstanding, and overall poor security posture. Considering that this relationship is so vital to the success or failure to a cybersecurity program, the entire security posture comes down to the relationship between two people. Without this understanding or at least attempt to work together, cybersecurity would be lacking across the organization.

CONCLUSION

People, process, and technology are objectives that reach across anyone in an IT or cybersecurity management position. From IT and cybersecurity leads to management and executives, two themes emerge as essential to meeting both groups' goals: communication and collaboration. Collaboration is based upon the ability to understand and appreciate each other's teams and concerns. Communication is genuinely based on listening and working together to accomplish goals. But the inability to work together can ultimately lead to problems with the cyber hygiene and could have farther reaching implications.

Very little is placed on the ability to have a positive relationship between layers of management. Asking team members how they feel about management, or how effective they are at accomplishing their goals, could be a good exercise for executives to take part in. And within understanding management relationships, the ability to collaborate between the executive leadership team is critical to the success of the business. This does not mean that executives need to know everything about the technology or cybersecurity implementations, but they need to have reliable staff and the ability to coordinate those efforts. An important note from this chapter is that cognitive limitations can have serious impact on how management teams operate with technical staff.

Cognitive limitations are not discussed within the IT or cybersecurity fields. Except for behavioral analysis teams, insider threat groups, or red teams, psychology terminology and phenomenon are not discussed in any detail. Cognitive limitations are based on the amount of information someone can ingest and provide actionable output within the context of that information. For example, how much information can a security analyst ingest with alerts and a constant stream of data, and actionably understand and determine the severity of each alert?

Relationships, communication, cognitive limitations, and competing goals increase the level of complexity within IT and cybersecurity teams. These layers of complexity can seriously damage the security posture within the organization. If team leads, management, and executives are unable to seriously analyze their relationships inside and outside of their groups, it can be devastating to the organization. Negative relationships or interactions could lead to misinformation, poor security posture, lack of customer functionality, and a host of other issues. Without the awareness of how interactions can impact technical infrastructure and cybersecurity operations, organizations would never fully reach maturity or grow their revenue and impact on their industry.

Chapter 8

Financial issues and responsibilities

IT BUDGETS

Budgets have been discussed at a minimum but require further investigation in relation to how IT and cybersecurity groups interact. Budget size will determine how many tools are available to them, what kind of resources or training they can take, as well as how large their team could be. IT budgets historically have been smaller or had to prioritize projects for highest improvement to the business for the lowest cost. In an IT operations environment, administrators may not be aware of the amount of money available for new tools or upgraded infrastructure. The cost of software and devices would be known to upper-level management and executives, although administrators and engineers may work on cost proposals for new projects or when upgrading current systems.

In the case of a new system or technology implementation, the cost of licensing, new equipment, or supporting infrastructure would be accounted for in the proposal. Project managers and management would also account for number of resources, personnel, and time required to perform associated work. However, the IT budget would more than likely not account of any cybersecurity initiatives or assessments within the project. For example, in the deployment of new mobile devices for the development team. The budget would account for the devices, licensing costs for development applications, monthly data costs, and any supporting infrastructure. Even if the project schedule accounted for security assessments and evaluations, it would most likely not provide a cost estimate for how long security tasking would take or associated personnel.

For systems upgrades, the associated costs would include decommissioning and removing old systems, as well as anything needed for licensing and new equipment. IT budgets are expansive and do not just support the applications and infrastructure for user productivity, but also mobile devices like laptops and tablets. Things like encryption, cloud services, Software as a Service (SaaS) products and Identity and Access Management (IAM) initiatives would all be covered under IT spending: personnel, resources, tools, and data centers and any Disaster Recovery (DR) hardware and software.

DOI: 10.1201/9781003264422-8

A DR set up may include a multi-cloud High Availability (HA) setup with one cloud infrastructure being the primary and having a failover secondary cloud provider as a backup. All of this to say, that IT budgets require a lot of thought and as business needs change, the infrastructure, applications, and other products all must adjust.

Regardless of the specific items under IT budgets, spending is focused on supporting business strategy, and what users need to achieve company mission and vision. For example, a sales team would require mobile devices, specialty applications, access to documents anywhere, and the ability to communicate across any device quickly and securely. Sales teams need to keep customer information confidential and stored safely, so this would be an area where IT and cybersecurity budgets may meet, although IT budgets may include encryption methods, Multi-Factor Authentication (MFA), and IAM without consideration or consultation with the cybersecurity team. Vendors or methods might be chosen that best align with the business, and even with a cybersecurity consult, ultimately products will be chosen to support the users.

And in most cases, if the IT budget is small and supports the users but not the IT staff that manage the technology, they will use open-source products to assist them. Using open-source software (OSS) can lead to a host of other issues, including security concerns or using an application that is managed infrequently by the developers. In many cases, OSS is managed by a few developers who update and patch vulnerabilities when they have time. Given the recent Log4Shell exploit nightmare, many organizations may be reconsidering how they use OSS and what implications the software supply chain has on them. But regarding an IT budget, OSS is one of the ways IT administrators can maneuver around lack of funding. The IT group may be lacking for funding, but almost always, the cybersecurity budget will be much smaller.

CYBERSECURITY BUDGETS

Cybersecurity budgets are much larger in the last year or two than they ever have been, given the recent Executive Orders by President Biden and the SolarWinds and Log4Shell exploits. Many large organizations have a sizeable budget for cybersecurity teams, to include threat hunting groups, Security Operations Centers (SOCs), security engineering teams, and Incident Response groups. But in a smaller organization, cybersecurity teams would be smaller and supporting several initiatives with few people and even less tools at their disposal. Cybersecurity analysts, like IT administrators, must be creative with their use of budget and spending for tools. Where Chief Information Security Officers (CISOs) exist, they manage the budget for the cybersecurity groups and determine what tools and resources are needed to support the organization.

Unfortunately, most cybersecurity teams and CISOs must pick the most important products and may leave gaps in visibility, meaning that a CISO could select an antimalware and analysis tool that is incredibly comprehensive, over selecting three products that may serve separate functions. Even with the antimalware and analysis tool though, the cybersecurity team would be missing another tool to conduct forensics investigations in the case of an incident and rely on OSS. Traditionally, cybersecurity budgets have been much smaller than IT budgets, leading to contention and in-fighting between the Chief Information Officer (CIO) and CISO. And in the case where the CISO reports to the CIO, they may be overridden on budgeting decisions, leading to ineffective cybersecurity programs. Fortunately, there are quite a few OSS tools and techniques that are available to cybersecurity teams and are leveraged to fill any security gaps.

Consider a cybersecurity team that is using most of their budget on one comprehensive threat hunting and Endpoint Detection and Response (EDR) tool, as well as a vulnerability scanning and reporting program. The CISO then reports to the CIO and determines that the current vulnerability scanning tool is not providing the best metrics for the cybersecurity team. The CISO recommends removing the current tool and implementing a new vulnerability scanning and reporting tool that provides more functionality and visibility. This additional visibility could detect unknown vulnerabilities and the ability to calculate risk more accurately and automatically. The CIO does not see a need to replace this tool because the IT team needs to implement a new encryption method and infrastructure to support it. The CIO does not approve the request and tells the CISO that they need to use the information they have available.

The decision to keep with the current vulnerability scanning and reporting software may limit the ability to find and act upon vulnerabilities. This limited visibility could be devastating to an organization if the cybersecurity team is unable to understand the risk holistically in the environment. Risk management is something that CIOs and CISOs must collaborate on, and the CIO should be looking to the CISO to provide objective information. Without awareness or ability to see the full threat landscape, a CISO would only be able to provide a best guess for what priorities the team should focus on. If there was a cyberattack leveraging one of the vulnerabilities that was not caught by the vulnerability scanning tool, the CISO may still be held responsible for not knowing about it. Even if it was the CIOs decision to ultimately deny the request for an increased budget for the vulnerability scanning software, the CISO is held accountable for cyberattacks.

This is one example of an interaction between a CIO and a CISO on the cybersecurity budgeting and potential implications. Consider the constant decisions around IT and cybersecurity spending, whether for tools or resources, and how the relationship between a CIO and CISO could impact the functionality or security of the environment. A cybersecurity budget is ultimately intended to protect the organization from cyberattacks or recover quickly. An IT budget is focused on the business strategy and ongoing operations of users. Given the already known differences in objectives between the teams, spending could cause tension between executives which would trickle down to their employees. Once employees find out about where money is being spent, teams may feel slighted by those decisions or that their concerns are not valid, which is another reason for burnout, frustration, and potentially leading to disgruntled employees.

IT TOOLS

Both IT and cybersecurity teams need tools, which is the *technology* component discussed earlier. For operations or engineering groups, tools assist in the automation and orchestration of manual tasks. These tools may also help provide insight into problems or troubleshooting complex issues within applications or on the network. There are many OSS tools available to help IT teams, but typically the ones that require a bit of the IT budget contain more functionality. The goal of using tools is to reduce overhead and administrative manual tasking. This allows for administrators and engineers to spend more time on troubleshooting complex issues or improving the environment.

For example, running a virtual desktop infrastructure there is a lot of latency when logging on to the desktop. It takes a user a full minute to log in and see the virtual desktop when it should only take 2–5 seconds for the desktop to load. An IT administrator is trying to determine the cause of this lag and what is happening between user authentication and loading the desktop. Since this is affecting all virtual desktop users, upper-level management have been notified and they what the issue resolved quickly. The administrator finds a script or a tool online that can run while a test desktop loads and will provide context for any services or processes that are lingering during startup. Without the tool, the administrator would have to look at logs, processes, services, encryption methods, antivirus settings, network settings, and more. The use of this tool helps to identify and resolve the problem quickly, allowing the IT administrator to focus on improving the infrastructure.

Another example of effective IT tools is the use of a network sniffing or analysis tool. When troubleshooting network problems or latency, something like Wireshark is essential to solve problems quickly. Whether determining if there is network latency between systems or the ability to capture and analyze packets offline, a network analysis tool as an IT administrator staple. For example, customers are seeing delays on a website hosted on two of the primary customer-facing web servers. Since this is an essential service and provides revenue for the organization, this becomes a top priority for the engineers. With the aid of a network analysis tool, they are quickly able to determine that those two servers had been put on a separate Virtual

LAN mistakenly. The use of this tool provides quick troubleshooting and little effort on the part of engineers freeing them up to continue other work.

Whether using open-source or paid tools, they can accumulate over time. The term "technical debt" enters the conversation as a point of contention between IT and cybersecurity teams. If administrators are allowed to install tools on privileged workstations or servers without automation or required versions, out-of-date and EOL tools can become a major issue. Consider a network with ten administrators, who can log in to multiple servers, applications, and services in the environment. They each install separate tools, some open-source and some paid for by the CIO budget, all at different version levels. As administrators take on additional responsibilities, new administrators come on to the team, and others leave without uninstalling applications, the number of vulnerabilities grows.

Another point of contention between IT and cybersecurity teams would be how to handle those vulnerabilities. IT administrators argue they need each individual tool to perform daily tasking and the cybersecurity team is concerned with the number of versions, EOL tools, and vulnerabilities noted on the tools. The cybersecurity teams recommend updating several of the tools to the latest version and removing other outdated and EOL tools. The IT administrators comply with the updates but are now frustrated by the limited tools available to automate tasks. The administrators feel they are spending more time now on manual tasks and have to spend more time updating tools, and the cybersecurity team feels like they are constantly checking admin servers for vulnerabilities.

CYBERSECURITY TOOLS

Cybersecurity teams typically rely on open-source tools to help identify potential attackers in the environment. With smaller budgets, security teams would have malware and antivirus identification and remediation software, vulnerability scanning and reporting tools, as well as network monitoring applications. These are the standard types of security tools, but larger organizations would also employ threat hunting and intelligence tools and tactics as well. Forensics tools are also an important component of any cybersecurity team, especially if they have a mature insider threat program. Without intimate knowledge of the several functions a cybersecurity team performs, other groups within the organization may not understand the need to purchase so many tools.

Cybersecurity teams, typically with a smaller budget, must be creative in their solutions when it comes to automation. Even with some of the more comprehensive security tools on the market, analysts and engineers must develop or find scripts to automate mundane tasks. As mentioned previously, conducting the same monotonous tasks over and over can become a reason for cybersecurity analysts to leave their roles. Automation becomes a key factor for both IT and cybersecurity retention for CIOs and CISOS. The encouragement of creative solutions or spending time to automate daily and weekly tasks can seriously improve relationships between executives, management, and technical staff. Products and services provided by cybersecurity companies are supplemented by open-source tools or scripts created by the technical Subject Matter Experts (SMEs).

An example of an open-source tool used by smaller security teams would be something to pull browser history from a user profile. Whether a malicious insider or a case of employee misuse, a cybersecurity analyst would need to have some forensic tools available. The area of forensics is a great example of the use of open-source software to aid in the identification or exfiltration of data from a workstation or device. A security analyst would deploy the use of a tool like BrowserHistory to investigate any browsers installed on the machine. Especially with a small cybersecurity team or IT operations groups who perform forensics tasks for investigations, free tools are essential.

As mentioned, there seems to still be gaps between how other teams perceive a cybersecurity teams skills, requirements to perform job functions, and the many domains within the field. This can lead to a lack of understanding on what tools may be necessary to perform work and could lead to cybersecurity teams needing to use a variety of open-source options. Open-source tools can be helpful but may be limited in what detail they provide to analysts. Without proper funding, cybersecurity teams may only see a portion of the information they need to make an informed decision on risk management. If IT and cybersecurity teams rely heavily on open-source tools to manage functionality and risk, they will be providing a best guess on where problems may exist.

IT SERVICES

IT groups provide a variety of services to an organization, including mobile device management (MDM), specialty application support, helpdesk, and initial troubleshooting basic issues, as well as engineering and architecture projects. With the onslaught of new technology and tools available to organizations, IT teams are constantly evaluating new software and ways of supporting users. Chatbots are incredibly popular to provide front-end support to users before they reach a helpdesk. This helps to cut down on some of the initial troubleshooting or questions that a helpdesk may receive. For example, a chatbot may inform users of an outage for a particular website or service within the organization, alleviating several requests to the helpdesk. IT services are evolving and maturing as more automation is available to support basic requests.

Within a smaller organization, IT services might include mobile device and cloud infrastructure support, data storage and permissions, and IAM-based responsibilities. This is not all inclusive but would be a basic group of services. IT groups may also support web applications for users or customers as well as internal communications and websites. In larger organizations,

IT services include network security, consultation, architecture and design, backup and data recovery, as well as HA services. Consultation could be internal performed by IT architects or externally to customers as a service. IT groups could provide internal or external support for products based on the user population and type of business.

IT services like backup and DR activities are incredibly essential for the business and can have a major impact in the case of a ransomware incident. If a ransomware attack hit an organization, for example, a business would need to quickly recover data and systems. Ransomware would lock out systems and limit ability for users to perform job functions. Due to the popularity of ransomware attacks, and since they are easier to perform for attackers, IT groups must be ready to perform recovery services. Other types of attacks like DDoS and malware could require rebuilding systems if there was little preparation done by IT and cybersecurity teams. This is a good example of where IT and cybersecurity teams would need to collaborate and work together when restoring service for users.

IT teams also provide operations and support services for mobile devices and applications. Consider an organization with scientists in the field who need access to specialty applications on their mobile devices to collect data. If the applications were to be unavailable or the mobile devices failed while in the field, this could impact the scientists work and time to upload pertinent data. IT teams would be running the backend infrastructure to support the mobile devices, better known as MDM, as well as the virtual applications. The MDM team would need to respond quickly to outages and be prepared to support field teams with their backup strategy and ability to restore any lost data.

These are only two examples of situations where IT provides services to users. IT teams are diverse in skillset and abilities, which are leveraged in high stress situations like outages or interrupted services. IT groups are under immense pressure to keep services available to users and are typically held to a Service Level Agreement (SLA) for uptime or availability. For example, an IT operations group might be responsible for keeping systems in the cloud environment up 99% of the time. This uptime might impact how they interact with cybersecurity groups, especially if security control changes or patches would affect that uptime. It is possible to have security or maintenance time built into a contract, but if not, operations would be considered more important than security in some cases.

CYBERSECURITY SERVICES

Cybersecurity teams provide a wide variety of services, although other groups may not have as much visibility to them. In the case of an outage for IT services, users and customers are aware of the teams working to resolve the issue. Users might be more familiar with helpdesk teams who resolve tickets for them or escalate to higher tiered engineers. Users may only interact with cybersecurity teams in the event of a spam email that downloaded malware, or when a user visits a malicious site. The interaction from users to IT staff is generally to resolve problems, whereas users interact with cybersecurity teams in a negative or risky situation. This can lead to fear or concern from users when they hear from the cybersecurity team that they downloaded malware or had to contain their machine because of an incident.

Cybersecurity groups provide continuous monitoring, vulnerability identification and remediation instruction, security alert monitoring, consultation, and engineering services. Continuous monitoring is typically done with the aid of a vulnerability scanning and monitoring tool, and reports are provided to systems and applications owners. Vulnerability identification would be done with reporting or configuring scans for systems owners. Remediation instructions would be provided to IT groups that needed assistance with prioritizing or resolving complex vulnerabilities. Security alert monitoring would be a constant activity to review automated alerts for network devices, endpoints, mobile devices, or applications. Consultation would be an internal or external function for vulnerabilities, remediation activities, software security reviews, or risk management. Engineering is a growing service where security engineers work with developers or create security solutions for the enterprise.

Security teams provide internal services to users, systems and applications owners, as well as executive management. They may be required to manage reports to outside agencies or provide evidence for audits. While not as tangible as IT teams, the services that cybersecurity teams offer to an organization are essential to support the organization. For example, if a catalog was available to show the available services for IT and cybersecurity groups, they would differ significantly. However, both teams provide invaluable support to the business strategy and users, regardless of the amount or type of service (Figure 8.1).

The important distinction between IT and cybersecurity services are the visibility to users and awareness of the organization. There are many functions between both groups that are unknown to the general population within a business. A user may only interact with a helpdesk or administrator and very rarely reach an engineer or higher tier of SME. And on the cybersecurity side a user would only interact with the SOC for an alert on their machine. Without a full understanding of the services that each team provides, users and even executives may not support or approve funding for associated tools and software. IT and cybersecurity teams do not always have the visibility to the organization for services and support they provide to the business.

IT PROJECTS

Because technology span all aspects of the organization, projects within IT groups could fall under innovation, engineering, development, or operations.

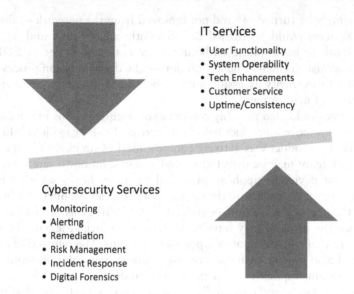

IT Services
- User Functionality
- System Operability
- Tech Enhancements
- Customer Service
- Uptime/Consistency

Cybersecurity Services
- Monitoring
- Alerting
- Remediation
- Risk Management
- Incident Response
- Digital Forensics

Figure 8.1 Difference between IT and cyber services.

Helpdesk, Tiered engineering groups, cloud architecture, and infrastructure are all areas with ongoing projects. Whether it is new hardware or software, application development, changing current technologies, or integrating new teams, IT groups are juggling multiple endeavors. These projects are more often including cybersecurity teams to either conduct reviews on bringing in new products, or for approvals to implement new systems into production. But there are multiple ways IT and cybersecurity groups would work together on IT projects.

When a new application, technology, or type of tool is going to be used in the environment, IT groups would provide initial recommendations. Depending on the industry, IT engineers could be required to evaluate two to three products of similar functionality for cost and ability to integrate into the infrastructure. For example, when looking for a new email client for users, they might need to evaluate Office 365, Google Mail Suite, and other products at the same time. Before purchasing a product, it would also need to pass the security team for an initial inspection into how secure the product is or could be. The security team may be called upon after the initial inspection of the email client and they would provide a risk management review.

Another example of an IT project with cybersecurity integration would be conducting application or device upgrades. It is possible in a situation like this, that the decommissioning of old products would be just as important as the integration of new systems. A security team would need to provide input into both aspects of the project, otherwise decommission of systems could go wrong in a multitude of ways. In some cases, servers and devices would simply be turned off and not removed from the network or domain. Those systems could be turned on accidently at any time and added to the network or back online without anyone realizing. Older or EOL systems could also accidently be left on during the decommission process, and without a full security assessment could be missed in the development and integration of new systems.

IT teams would also possibly consult cybersecurity teams in the event of the need to remove a product based on increased risk or exploitability. For example, if a product was actively compromised by an exploit in the product, the IT team may be directed to find a new solution to replace it. This replacement device or application would be under heavy scrutiny by the cybersecurity team to ensure the removal of the older product and installation of the new one was done securely. A situation like this carries increased risk since the product may have to be removed quickly, leaving IT teams without monitoring or required operations systems. The removal of a product could also impact customers or users, and a new solution would need to be determined quickly. Security teams would need to provide validation of the new solution and potentially assist IT teams with the installation and configuration.

IT and cybersecurity must collaborate closely for IT endeavors to succeed. Without open communication and including security from the onset of projects, IT project fail. But this is larger than the failure of a project, it could also lead to major insecurities throughout the organization. If security is not included in initial assessment of a product, it could be approved and installed in the environment before the security team finds out. Once they identify this insecure product, it is already too late and has been integrated in the infrastructure. This makes it much more difficult to remove it or to find an alternate solution, especially since replacing it would be costly. IT and cybersecurity collaboration is essential to the success and security of IT projects.

CYBERSECURITY PROJECTS

Given that cybersecurity is made up of so many domains, security projects are vast and touch every area of the organization. Like IT projects, security teams would need to communicate and understand the infrastructure before selecting products. Security teams would be involved in security assessments, implementing new security tools, threat hunting and intelligence gathering, compliance exercises, and many more projects. Cybersecurity projects differ from their IT counterparts in the way that projects carry a major risk to the security of the organization. If not executed properly, it could impact the overall security of the network or increase risk the environment. Security teams must balance functionality and security in the deployment of new tools.

For example, cybersecurity groups that would be working to implement a new EDR solution would have to be cautious not to accidently block machines or affect users' applications. If not configured properly, an EDR client could block someone's machine from internet access, or automatically contain itself if it thought it found malware, instead of notifying the SOC before containment. Without working with the IT team to understand how EDR may impact servers and other systems, there could be widespread functionality issues. If misconfigured or not tailored to collect enough information or alert on events would also create ineffective security. If an IT or security team configured it without the other's input, functionality or security would be a major concern.

Another example of a potential issue in security projects would be the creation and enforcement of a DevSecOps program. This program would require security engineers to be involved with development projects at the onset, during, and at the conclusion of the project. During initial phases, security teams would provide input for secure development practices and guidance for secure settings. Security would also be involved at 2-week check-ins, or stage-gate reviews, to discuss current misconfigurations or identification of new security concerns. And at the end of a project, the security team would be able to provide a final assessment and sign off on the project as ready for production. Without the integration of security during critical stages of the development process, an assessment at the end could mean failure for the entire product. Or it could mean a product was deployed to users or customers without a security assessment and is rife with vulnerabilities and missing controls (Figure 8.2).

One of the concerns with cybersecurity projects is that they may run in combination or in parallel with IT projects. It is possible with a smaller budget or without additional resources, cybersecurity projects may be more difficult to receive approvals to begin or they may be delayed because

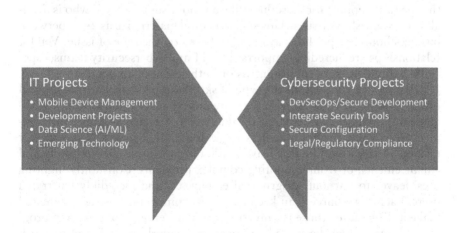

Figure 8.2 Cyber vs IT projects.

of other IT endeavors. Cybersecurity teams may be forced to implement open-source tools as an intermediary step while waiting to purchase or obtain more comprehensive software. There may also be technical and operational concerns that delay cybersecurity software being deployed into production. For example, if the IT team is in the middle of a mail migration, they may hold off on implementing a new EDR solution. And this could be for several reasons, one being that it is easier to troubleshoot one new technology than two at the same time.

IT and cybersecurity may also work together on new security projects like network micro-segmentation for the network, Public Key Infrastructure (PKI) integration, or updating encryption methods. Security teams may also need IT support for supporting infrastructure requirements, alignment with current IT tooling, or troubleshooting configuration issues. For example, if there was an issue noted in the Citrix infrastructure with logons, the IT operations team may work with the cybersecurity team to see if antivirus, anti-malware, or EDR solutions could be the root cause. If the cybersecurity team does not think there is an issue, or vice versa, this could impact the amount of time to troubleshoot and ultimately resolve a ticket. IT teams are highly focused and impacted by the time to resolve issues, and if cybersecurity teams did not work well with them, this could lead to disagreement and distrust between the two teams.

IT RESOURCES

Larger IT teams have a wide array of resources available for projects and engineering tasks, including personnel, vendors, and supporting teams. Resources could be the employees on the various IT teams or the types of tools and technology at their disposal. A resource could be a contact that they have as support for a product, like a vendor support SME who is available to troubleshoot issues. This support could materialize as 24/7, between business hours, or per hour availability based on the type of issue. Vendor relationships are incredibly important for IT and cybersecurity teams, especially in high pressure environments or in the event of an outage.

Resources can also mean the type of skills and personnel at the disposal of the IT team. If there were only two senior systems administrators available and a handful of helpdesk technicians to manage an entire environment, this would mean limited resources to handle operations and project tasking. A situation like this leaves little time for projects, environmental enhancements, or troubleshooting complex problems. Constantly 'fighting fires' leaves to burnout, disgruntled employees, and incredibly frustrated users. Lack of resources can keep an IT environment in a steady state and make it difficult for those running systems and services to make any progress. IT teams may be forced to consistently work extra hours to reach milestones for projects or spend extra hours on conferences with vendors sending logs and screenshots.

Varying skillsets on a team can mean the difference between project success and failure. If an IT team has no one with cloud architecture knowledge, they would be lacking in the resources to successfully migrate to the cloud. But if an organization paid for training for employees to upskill, they would have the available resource for knowledge and eventually trained skill. Available training for employees can be a valuable resource for the employees and provides knowledge to perform tasks as well as the ability for an employee to grow in their career. The topic of available resources to teams includes both paid for and provided opportunities for employees. Resources are not a linear or flat concern throughout the environment, and it can be incredibly powerful to provide the appropriate resources for IT teams.

But if IT teams are small, they can adapt with open-source tools and software to fill some gaps in knowledge or automation. There has been a recent boom of repositories like Github and increased vendor-specific and vendor-agnostic publicly available forums for troubleshooting guidance. These open forums allow engineers, administrators, and architects in the IT space to collaborate and share information to troubleshoot issues. There are also several open-source scripts and add-on tools that can help with automation, provide troubleshooting support, or even help resolve issues based on prior administrator's experience.

CYBERSECURITY RESOURCES

With traditionally smaller budgets and fewer resources available, cyber-security teams (as well as small IT teams) are used to working with more open-source resources. As mentioned in previous sections, some security tools may be managed by IT teams, like EDR or antivirus. Without the ability to manage the tools themselves, security teams must coordinate changes and alterations with IT operations. Cybersecurity resources would include any alerting or continuous monitoring software, threat hunting or intelligence gathering tools, and forensics applications. Resources would also include the personnel on cybersecurity teams whether analysts, engineers, or a combination of the two. Cybersecurity teams are quite varied in skillsets and abilities but are typically a mix of GRC and technical personnel.

A varied skillset is an invaluable resource on a cybersecurity team. Technical skills include software development, ethical hacking or penetration testing, automation and design, as well as the ability to manage and integrate new devices and software. Non-technical skills are incredibly valuable to a cybersecurity team, including conducting security assessments and audits, understanding and implementing policy and guidance, as well as project management and organization. Soft skills, emotional intelligence, empathy, and understanding for other teams and goals are unspoken resources that could mean the success of a cybersecurity project. The discussion of empathy and emotional intelligence is growing in leadership circles, but this empathy comes in as a great resource for cybersecurity teams to collaborate and work well with IT teams.

Without empathy, cybersecurity teams would find it incredibly difficult to create (and keep) a secure network. For example, without empathy for an IT operations administrator who manages multiple systems and is already working overtime, cybersecurity teams would never be able to implement controls. The security analyst sends threatening emails to the administrator about missing security controls and without much guidance. The administrator immediately goes to their manager and says that they have little information to go on and do not have the bandwidth to deal with these security controls. IT management goes to their counterparts within cybersecurity and complains about the lack of information and coordination from their analysts. In this scenario, no one wins, and security controls will sit unconfigured. IT administrators and security analysts alike will be frustrated and create tension between the teams.

But there are plenty of technical resources available for cybersecurity teams to help achieve automation and implementation of mitigating controls. The cybersecurity community is full of individuals who share information openly and freely, like the way IT engineers share troubleshooting information in forums. Cybersecurity analysts, researchers, and engineers use social media, blogs, and streaming services to share open-source information to each other. This is very similar to how developers share code with Github and provide it freely to other developers. Free cybersecurity resources are quite vast and were created out of the necessity for free and easily available information. With the large number of domains within cybersecurity, tools and other resources are essential for each area.

IT GOALS

One of the major areas of concern and contention between IT and cybersecurity teams are the goals for each group. There is such a stark contrast between these goals, that it can lead to fighting for priority and resources to meet those goals. IT teams would need to meet several goals, but the primary goal being to support the CIO office and all users with a set uptime. Whether operations, engineering, or architecture and design, IT teams are focused on the goals set by the CIO's office. Based on the type of users the team supports, their goals may vary quite widely, and may even have competing priorities. To understand how these individual missions may clash with cybersecurity teams, a few examples of IT teams will be explored.

The first example is the IT operations group in charge of managing the operations of a cloud infrastructure. This team manages the policies, baseline templates, automation, OS and application levels of a number of servers. These servers cover a variety of functions, including customer-facing shopping websites and the internal operations for users. This team also manages the IAM policies and other configuration settings for the cloud infrastructure. They are required to keep an uptime of services to both users and customers at 99%, which means that they do not have a maintenance window and have built in a lot of HA to keep systems available during patching cycles and reboots. When security settings are requested to be installed, they are not considered a top priority, unless mandated by the CISO or enforced by that group.

Another example of an IT team with potentially competing priorities is a network engineering team that manages the network throughout the environment. They also have a 99% SLA to keep systems and sites available for users. With users across the United States, they have many networks that require constant management and alerting to be sure that no branch sites lost availability. The network team is constantly balancing operations tasks with implementing improvements to the environment as well. When they receive notice from the security team that there are critical vulnerabilities on their network devices, the team must now prioritize which tasks are done first. And if it takes days or a week to test and implement the changes in production, this means that any other enhancements are delayed by at least a week.

A final example of IT teams who may have competing priorities with cybersecurity groups are junior and senior personnel within a helpdesk team. With an in-house helpdesk and systems administration team, their ultimate goal is to close tickets within a certain time period, as defined by the CIO. Helpdesk technicians must solve problems or escalate to the next tier within 15 minutes, and second- and third-level systems administrators and engineers must resolve problems within a week or explain when it can be completed. The upper tiers may take weeks or months to resolve highly complex issues but would need to provide continuous status updates to upper-level management on open tickets. When security issues are identified or patches need to be applied to production systems, the helpdesk and tiered team would be concerned about any impact to open tickets. They would also be concerned about how security patches could impact users and potentially create more tickets for the helpdesk to manage and close.

CYBERSECURITY GOALS

Cybersecurity goals stand in complete contrast to operations and IT teams. IT teams, as seen in the previous scenarios, are focused on uptime, closing tickets, or making sure users always have systems and applications available. Cybersecurity teams are engrossed in audit results, conducting security assessments, working on penetration tests and reports, or continuous monitoring and vulnerability management programs. And while these are only a few of the goals of cybersecurity teams, the main focus is to ensure the security of the organization. Security spans across secure configuration, passing audits, and ultimately preventing cybersecurity attacks. And while most cybersecurity teams are aware that an incident is likely to occur at any time, they are working toward prevention, detection, and recovery of systems in the event of an incident.

For example, an SOC would be focused on the monitoring for potential threats, malware detection, or even searching for IOCs with the security tools at their disposal. The SOC would contain or quarantine machines with infections, investigate potential malicious actor network scanning, and monitoring EDR alerts for malware or viruses. If there is an IOC identified with an APT group on a workstation, SOC analysts would be quick to quarantine or contain that machine. They would most likely reach out to the user and notify them, but IT teams may not be notified initially. Since helpdesk technicians and SOC analysts typically have separate tracking methods for tickets and cases, there could be lack of awareness when a case like this occurs. Helpdesk and IT teams may be notified after management chains have been told and may be fielding calls from users asking why their machines are not accessible. This could lead to extra calls to the helpdesk, inability to resolve the issue, or the technician could remove containment on the machine if they did not have notes for the incident.

Another area of differing goals for IT and cybersecurity are for security assessors/auditors who conduct security assessments. A security assessor/auditor may have several assessments to perform in a year, with deadlines for each one. For example, security assessors/auditors may have two assessments to perform each quarter, including collecting evidence, writing reports, and resolving vulnerabilities and configuration settings. For each assessment, the security assessor/auditor may need to work with different IT groups and systems owners and review separate environments. A security assessor/auditor would need to understand a variety of security frameworks and requirements, and what controls apply to each technology. With tight deadlines and a variety of documentation needed to perform the assessments, security assessors/auditors would need frequent contact with the systems owners. Without quick responses, security assessors/auditors might leave out information in the assessment or be unable to perform a complete review of the system. This can lead to gaps in security or inaccurate reporting of risk management concerns.

Another cybersecurity goal that may contrast with IT objectives is conducting penetration tests to determine what security controls are missing or what exploitable vulnerabilities exist. A penetration tester would provide a list of what they would like to accomplish, typically in a Rules of Engagement document. This document would contain which systems, networks, and physical security areas they would use to conduct attacks. The IT team would have an opportunity to come back and state if any networks or systems are off-limits and are not part of the test. However, if the IT team is not willing to allow the penetration testers to perform their work or access certain areas of the network, this would limit their findings. If the penetration testing team and the IT team are unable to compromise or work together, the security team would be unable to provide a comprehensive report.

IT VERSUS CYBERSECURITY

As seen in a variety of areas, including resources, projects, and goals, IT and cybersecurity teams may have a difficult time working together if they have different priorities. The biggest lesson from this chapter should be the incredible differences between the teams. IT teams may have a larger budget, more resources, but also more responsibility when it comes to uptime and customer support. Cybersecurity teams are focused on the security of systems and the network, whereas IT teams are focused on keeping systems online and supporting users. And if executive leadership and management do not support and understand each other's goals, it is incredibly difficult to achieve anything in either department. With competing goals and priorities, it pins IT and cybersecurity teams against each other, instead of building a community with shared goals (Figure 8.3).

Something as simple as lack of coordination in an annual security assessment, could lead to major gaps in cybersecurity and unknown risks. It is incredibly difficult to get a holistic picture of the risks in an organization if security assessments are incomplete or the teams do not work well together. Something as simple as pushing off meetings and not responding to emails from security assessors/auditors to system owners, could lead to unpatched vulnerabilities. If the security assessor/auditor is specifically asking for evidence of a Group Policy Object and the IT team does not respond or

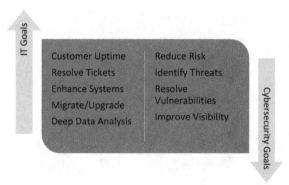

Figure 8.3 IT vs cyber goals.

provide a screenshot, they may fail part of the assessment. Even if the security assessor/auditor did not want to fail the system owner, they may have no choice based on the scoring system within the report.

A failed security assessment could lead to even further consequences, including increased pressure from management. IT management may go back to the security team to pressure them to change the failure to a passing rating, given they provide the evidence quickly. The security team may receive negative feedback from the CIO's team because they failed a system without working more cohesively with the IT team. A situation like this can lead to frustration, lack of trust between the teams, and contention in future interactions. Even if each team had the best intentions throughout the project, an issue like this could have long-lasting effects on the ability for teams to work together. It would also lead to missed security controls, unresolved vulnerabilities, and a host of other security concerns.

Chapter 9

Education gaps between IT and cybersecurity

INTRODUCTION

As noted in other chapters, there are a variety of reasons for contention and misunderstandings between teams. Differing missions, project types, and availability of resources can all play a part in why these teams miscommunicate. But there are more areas for concern between IT and cybersecurity teams, specifically in education and training. IT and cybersecurity receive different types of education, whether academic or provided by technical vendors. Even in IT, depending on what professional track is taken, training and certifications can vary wildly. These wide arrays of skills are essential to creating a well-rounded IT team but could provide another avenue for misunderstandings.

It is not assumed that all IT and cybersecurity education and training would be the same in any profession. However, there are basic types of academic degrees and certifications in each industry. For example, a Helpdesk technician may have no college education, and one or two industry certifications to supplement. An IT administrator may have a computer science degree but no industry certifications. A security architect may hold 20 industry certifications across security and IT domains and a Doctorate degree. With this wide range of education and skillsets, every scenario cannot be discussed in detail here. But what is important in this section is that exploring some educational differences between IT and cybersecurity could lead us to understand why there may be a communication and technology gap.

Certifications are a hotly debated topic between both the IT and cybersecurity industries. On one side of the fence, people believe that anyone in IT should have at least one industry certification, and possibly several if they want to prove their skills to employers. Employers may put down a certain set of certifications as required on job descriptions, which means you would need the certification to be considered for the position. On the other side of the fence are incredibly talented and technical people in the industry who do not feel you need certifications to prove technical chops. They consider certifications to be unnecessary to prove technical skill and expensive to

DOI: 10.1201/9781003264422-9

individuals who may have to purchase training or other materials to support their studies and credentials. Regardless of where individuals sit in this debate, there are still several positions that require certifications.

IT CERTIFICATIONS

There are numerous certifications within the IT sector that are both vendor-specific and vendor-agnostic. Organizations like Microsoft, Amazon Web Services (AWS), and Citrix have multiple levels of certification available for administrators, engineers, and senior management. For example, within Microsoft there are various certification paths for developers, solution architects, data engineers and scientists, and administrators (Microsoft, n.d.). For the purposes of this section, groups like network engineers, database administrators, and systems engineers will also be considered part of the IT sector. With such a wide array of roles and requirements in IT, vendor-agnostic certifications are also available from technical trainers which cover topics for project managers and helpdesk technicians.

More academic institutions are also offering training and certifications to complement their technical degrees. For example, a degree in computer science might also have an elective available for Microsoft server administration that includes an entry level Microsoft certification. This is a major benefit for IT students because they do not necessarily have to choose between higher-level education and certification but pursue both in tandem. The ability to achieve certifications within technical programs is still relatively new in the industry and was not always available in the last 5–10 years. Certifications offered by universities could either be vendor-specific or something more general like the CompTIA A+ or Network+ certifications (CompTIA, n.d.).

There is also some debate in the industry about theoretical or concept-based certifications versus being certified in a specific technology. For IT generalists, they may hold certifications in a variety of technologies, like Microsoft server (latest version), AWS administrator, and Cisco Certified Network Professional (CCNP) (Cisco, n.d.). But someone who is an IT specialist may choose to focus on a certification path for a specific technology, like the data scientist path for AWS including Machine Learning, Database, and Data Analytics. IT management may choose to focus more on a Project Management Professional (PMP) or an Information Technology Infrastructure Library (ITIL) technical management certification. But certifications and the ability to attain them may be based on training budget available for employees, as well as if their company is supportive and encourages time to study.

Recommended and recognized certifications have been changing yearly, and even reviewing latest references on best IT certifications, the EC-Council's Certified Ethical Hacker (CEH) is shown as increasing in popularity (EC-Council, n.d.). However, this recommendation is confusing, because IT groups do not necessarily need to focus on ethical hacking. There is still disagreement and confusion about what certifications are best in an IT group, which can lead anyone in the IT field to look more at job descriptions for guidance than online articles and blogs. Job descriptions show everything from a bachelor's degree requirement to ITIL certifications for IT management positions. But IT contractor positions may require at least one industry certification to support contract requirements. It is relatively common for network engineering positions to require at least one networking certification for the devices in their environment, for example, a Cisco Networking certification.

Issues between IT and cybersecurity teams may arise with the amount of security training provided within IT certification programs. With the wide spread of IT certifications available, whether highly technical or management focused, it is not common for cybersecurity to be part of the training or exams. There might be some security measures or guidance provided within the training, but it is not a major part of the program. For example, a server OS certification course would not include what security controls match CIS benchmarks or NIST SP 800-53. Technical certifications focus on the technical implementation or management of a specific type of technology, and not necessarily how it would be securely configuration. Without baseline knowledge on what secure configuration might mean, IT and cybersecurity teams may disagree on how to implement a security framework.

CYBERSECURITY CERTIFICATIONS

Cybersecurity certifications span so many different areas, including threat intelligence, data analysis, digital forensics, GRC, and security engineering and architecture. While several security certifications were initially vendor-agnostic, like the Certified Information Systems Security Professional (CISSP) and Security+, more vendors are releasing security-focused certifications. Businesses like Microsoft, Cisco, and Amazon have started creating security specialist certifications for their various applications and devices. The focus on security allows for more job positions in cybersecurity domains that focus on specific technologies and allow analysts and engineers to show their expertise to potential employers. But cybersecurity certifications which are vendor-agnostic are still very popular to show a wide range of skill and the ability to implement best practices across any technology.

The ability to get a certification in threat intelligence displays an individual's specific skillset within cybersecurity. Cybersecurity is a massive industry with many specializations and job roles. For a threat intelligence certification, for example, an individual would be able to show their expertise in research, intelligence gathering and organization, as well as the ability to review and analyze data quickly and efficiently. But a threat intelligence certification does not pigeon-hole an analyst into one position, they would also be highly skilled as a security analyst, security engineer, or in any role where they need to quickly gather and parse through large data sets. Not to mention they would probably be great on a red team if they were interested in learning offensive security. Skills learned in training and certification programs can be transferred to other positions with relative ease.

The only issue with learning vendor-agnostic certifications is that they do not include specific technical implementations for an application or device. While documentation would be available from the vendor, a certification like CISSP would not include step-by-step instruction for creating a secure environment. But a certification like CISSP is more meant to show expertise and to be considered an SME in cybersecurity. This is where vendor-specific certifications can complement a vendor-neutral option such as CISSP or CEH. Anything security-centric from AWS, Microsoft, or Cisco is complementary to CISSP or OSCP to show theoretical as well as practical knowledge. Some certifications do provide technical and hands-on experience with tools, like nmap or Wireshark, like the CEH or the Offensive Security Certified Professional (OSCP). The OSCP is a technical exam that requires the use of several tools and techniques and is completed by writing a report provided by Offensive Security (Offensive Security, n.d.).

There are plenty of options available within the cybersecurity certification world to show breadth and depth of knowledge. However, cybersecurity certifications do not provide instruction on what it means to be in IT operations and dealing with outages, Service Level Agreements (SLAs), or customer tickets. If someone has a background in IT operations and engineering and moves into cybersecurity, they will have the knowledge from a professional standpoint. But if someone receives only cybersecurity certifications and only works in cybersecurity, they may not have the same understanding or empathy for their IT counterparts. And the same goes for only receiving training in IT or education within the IT space, it could be difficult to understand what it means to work day-to-day in the cybersecurity world.

IT HIGHER EDUCATION

Academic IT programs from undergraduate up to doctoral programs have been around for some time. Although the original IT programs at academic institutions were called computer science, computer programming, or software engineering. More recently, IT programs have expanded and provide many areas of expertise including web development and design, video game design, cloud engineering, network operations, and IT management. It is possible to achieve either a relatively general degree in IT or a more specialized degree in networking, design, or management. Most universities, community colleges, and online institutes have at least one IT program, and many universities are solely dedicated to technical professions. Since IT has been a field of study for many more years than cybersecurity, there is quite a variety of options available for anyone interested in IT or software development.

A number of these IT programs include specialties or concentrations in a specific technology, like cloud engineering, IT management, network administration, software engineering, and supply chain management. There is also the newer field of OT which is also rising in popularity with degree programs from undergraduate to the doctoral level. As mentioned, there is still quite a debate in the IT industry on whether individuals need a degree for an entry-level position, like a helpdesk technician. Wherever one sits on the debate, there is clear value for achieving anything from an associate degree to a technical certification. It provides a background and initial methodologies for technical implementation, operations management, and troubleshooting styles. There is a mix of IT job listings that state that an associate or bachelor's degree is preferred, but not required.

While an IT degree is beneficial for engineering and analyst positions, it is certainly not a requirement or a 'must-have' item to a successful IT career. However, IT degrees do not necessarily include cybersecurity courses or training. But many college institutions provide cybersecurity as a concentration to any IT degree. This means that anyone would have the opportunity to take two or three focused electives in cybersecurity and provide complimentary knowledge to the IT degree. However, how many individuals take these cybersecurity courses out of the greater population of IT degrees that move into the technical field. It is certainly an option for students to learn about cybersecurity and would provide a good background for empathy between IT operations and cybersecurity groups.

CYBERSECURITY HIGHER EDUCATION

Cybersecurity programs in universities and community colleges have exploded in the last 5 years. Originally, a student could add a concentration in information assurance onto an IT or computer science degree. Students could also pursue an information assurance certificate or would have to compensate with a Security+ certification. Now, there are cybersecurity, risk management, cyberpsychology, threat intelligence, and digital forensics degrees from associate's up to the doctoral level. There are more specialties released from universities every year, including OT security, cyber investigations, cryptocurrency security, and cyber warfare. With the increased need for cybersecurity specialists across all industries, universities are creating unique and specialized programs to fit those needs. A number of these degrees can be done as a full program, or as a concentration onto a computer science or cybersecurity program.

Students have a variety of options available to choose from in the cybersecurity field; however, because a number of these programs are new or in their infancy, the material may not be comprehensive. There have been some questions in the industry whether cybersecurity degrees are not preparing students for a career in cybersecurity since this field is constantly changing. There is also debate on whether a cybersecurity degree is entirely necessary for a security analyst or engineer position. This is another point between the IT and cybersecurity industries that practitioners do not believe higher-level education is necessary to perform tasking. But academic institutions teach theory, frameworks, styles of thinking, and problem-solving for complex issues. A cybersecurity degree can provide the foundational knowledge required for a career in cybersecurity.

Even at higher levels of education like a graduate or doctoral-level program, students can learn management, research, and more comprehensive methodologies to bring into their professions. A negative outlook on education only provides more contention between practitioners either within their industry or between IT and cybersecurity. For example, if an IT group collectively looked down on the cybersecurity team for having bachelor's degrees, this would lead to friction and potentially difficult when collaborating on projects.

IT TRAINING OPTIONS

With the wide range of IT certifications available, a selection of training organizations has been established to help professionals attain certificates or certifications. These training groups provide access to online training and labs, in-person events for organizations or at off-site venues, and the ability to test after completing a course. Programs might include training, training and exams, materials, and assessments related to the topic. For example, a bootcamp style class may be a 4–5-day on-site training that includes three certification exams during that week. These training organizations either do vendor-agnostic training or work with businesses like Microsoft and AWS to provide training material for their exams. There are also numerous free online resources for certifications on streaming services or other online platforms.

But with the numerous options available, it can be difficult to discern which programs are comprehensive and provide accurate and up-to-date information. A concerning example is if there are 100 training vendors that provide training for one certification, what material are they using? There is no guarantee that even in one certification or accreditation program that individuals are getting a similar level of education. The problem of certification training goes deeper than simply that amount that are available, but the quality of education received by trained and certified IT professionals. If there are limited funds provided to employees, they may seek out free or relatively inexpensive options for certifications. Not all inexpensive options are bad, but the concern is inconsistency of material.

One of the benefits of a wide variety of training options for IT professionals is that there are many options available. While it can be difficult to discern how comprehensive the training would be, the ability to receive free or inexpensive training allows for both young professionals and career-switchers access to IT. However, IT training options do not necessarily cover cybersecurity objectives. For example, a training course on Windows systems administration might have a section on secure configuration if it is a several day bootcamp. A 1-hour training video or 1 day session may not have the time to cover cybersecurity requirements. This is where, like academic institutions, there is an option to learn about cybersecurity, but it is not a requirement.

CYBERSECURITY TRAINING OPTIONS

Like IT, there are a ton of options available for cybersecurity certification and domain-specific training. With the more recent boom of cybersecurity positions across industries, cybersecurity training organizations are growing to meet the needs of the industry. Like the concentrations available at academic institutions, training is available on threat intelligence, digital forensics, cybersecurity management, and risk management. From entry-level to complex topics, cybersecurity training is changing and growing as quickly as the field is. There are several well-respected security trainers available like SANS, ISC2, Coursera, and Udemy. However, some of these training options are incredibly expensive and out of reach for many young people in the industry.

Some higher-level training would instruct on ethical hacking concepts or security analysis, while more in-depth courses would cover topics like privilege escalation for Windows or Linux. Organizations like Udemy and Coursera provide massive libraries on high-level and more in-depth concepts, including courses for entry-level positions or executives. There are also many podcasts and individuals who post on social media covering cybersecurity topics. There are free resources available for anyone looking to become a cybersecurity professional or improve their skills once in the cybersecurity industry. But like the IT industry, with the amount of online training programs available, it can be difficult to identify the valuable and accurate programs. Without a training budget provided to employees, individuals would use free or inexpensive options to prepare for cybersecurity positions.

The cybersecurity industry is full of experts who openly share information on social media or provide mentorship to bring individuals into entry-level positions. Because there is such a need for cybersecurity professionals, training is a critical component to bringing people into the field. However, cybersecurity training programs do not cover IT operations or engineering tasking or skillsets. For example, within a cybersecurity course on digital forensics, the topic of how pulling forensics data would not include how it affects users or IT infrastructure. One of the items covered in forensics is the need to keep systems online and not shut down, to not lose pertinent data. However, this may contrast with the needs for containment or shutting down a system that is infected with ransomware or malware. Training within cybersecurity domains may even differ from each other and provide a separate point of view even within cybersecurity teams.

VENDOR-AGNOSTIC CERTIFICATIONS

Whether in the IT or cybersecurity field, vendor-agnostic certifications provide a great avenue for foundational knowledge. Certifications like ITIL, CompTIA Network+ or A+, and the Certificate of Cloud Security Knowledge (CCSK) are excellent options for entry- and mid-level positions. These types of certifications provide a base layer of information for both technical and non-technical professionals. They also show possible employers that individuals have initial and theoretical knowledge to apply to any technology and are not skilled in one specific technology. It allows for individuals to take the certifications and apply them to multiple technologies. For example, the CCSK would show employers that they have cloud knowledge and could apply those principles to AWS, GCP, or Azure.

A security analyst who received a Security+ certification would be qualified to work in several entry-level up to mid-level positions. To move up to a more high-level role in cybersecurity, a CISSP or CISSP concentration like ISSEP or ISSAP would meet requirements for security engineers or architects (ISC2, n.d.). Just as the ITIL foundations certification would be good for an IT team lead, the higher-level ITIL certifications would be more appropriate for IT or program managers. Certifications like CISSP or CEH are used in job descriptions or match the DoD requirements as mentioned in the DoD 8570 baseline certifications document (DoD Cyber Exchange Public, n.d.). Each level of Information Assurance Technician or Manager has associated certifications.

But vendor-agnostic certifications on their own may be better for IT or cybersecurity generalist positions, although at any level. If IT or cybersecurity specialists are focused in one type of technology, it would make sense to have both vendor-agnostic and vendor-specific certifications. For example, an IT administrator who manages cloud environments might start with the CCSK and then move to AWS certifications to complement one another. On the cybersecurity side, someone might start with the CySA+ and then work on audit certification like the ISACA Certified Information Security Auditor (CISA) to move into a security assessor or auditor role (Figure 9.1).

VENDOR-SPECIFIC CERTIFICATIONS

Focusing on a specific technology can help both IT and cybersecurity professionals show a depth of knowledge into one type of product. Someone

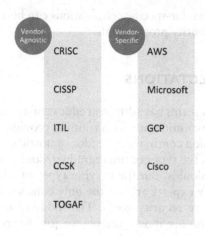

Vendor-Agnostic	Vendor-Specific
CRISC	AWS
CISSP	Microsoft
ITIL	GCP
CCSK	Cisco
TOGAF	

Figure 9.1 Vendor-agnostic vs vendor-specific certifications.

who is interested in Windows server administration might start with the Windows Server Administration Fundamentals certification and work up to the Microsoft Certified Systems Administrator (MCSA) (Microsoft, n.d.): Windows Server certification. It is common for cloud administrators and engineers to follow certification path focused on the Cloud Service Provider (CSP) used within their organization. Cloud administration or engineering positions may require at least one specific vendor-specific certification for entry- to mid-level job descriptions.

Cybersecurity professionals do not have as many vendor-specific certifications available, but the list is growing as the industry grows. As mentioned previously, organizations like Microsoft and AWS are providing security-centric certifications, but they may only have one or two available at this time. The hope is that more vendors will provide more cybersecurity certifications for their various products, instead of only one or two available for industry professionals. Since a number of these certifications are still new, it is still unseen if IT professionals will seek out these certifications to complement their IT-centric certifications. This is an area that the data is still not available for but is important to understand how much crossover there is between IT and cybersecurity certifications.

It is more likely that an individual who started in the IT operations field would have some IT certifications before they moved into the cybersecurity field. It is more often seen that individuals turn from IT positions into the cybersecurity field but is certainly possible that cybersecurity professionals would transition into an IT role. Vendor-specific IT certifications when moving into a cybersecurity role are incredibly beneficial for securing those products within an organization. Individuals with vendor-specific certifications understand the technology in-depth and have the capabilities to provide secure configuration guidance or mitigating controls. But the combination of vendor-agnostic or vendor-specific certifications can be an incredible asset to both IT and cybersecurity professionals.

INDUSTRY EXPECTATIONS

IT and cybersecurity teams have different educational backgrounds, whether from an academic institution or with a training provider for industry certifications. The discussion continues to vendor-agnostic or vendor-specific certifications as well as the types of undergraduate and graduate-level degrees available for professionals. But the varying types of education available to IT and cybersecurity experts are not the only concern when teams need to collaborate to achieve security goals. The industry dictates what certifications and education are most valuable for job descriptions and requirements. Depending on the sector, education or certifications may carry more weight and would be considered more highly regarded.

With the industries at odds for what certifications, training, or education is appropriate for job requirements, there is a lot of discord between the IT and cybersecurity fields. IT professionals may not believe any higher-level education is necessary, and cybersecurity teams may be more interested in graduate-level and vendor-agnostic certifications. Disagreements on what education is appropriate may lead to discord between teams and leave IT and cybersecurity teams at odds for collaboration. For example, an IT team does not believe any academic education is necessary, and industry certifications are superior for proving technical abilities. The cybersecurity team at the same organization values cybersecurity degrees and encourages new hires to work on certifications but they are not requirement. A situation like this may lead the IT team to not trust the knowledge of the cybersecurity team, leading to mistrust and not addressing their security concerns.

While that may seem like an extreme example, it is prevalent throughout both industries. Individuals may look down upon higher-level education and consider those with graduate-level or doctoral degrees to be non-technical. At the same time, anyone with a higher-level degree might look down upon technical employees who have no academic degree. This inability to have empathy or understanding for why another person has chosen an education path can lead to lack of cohesion and, ultimately, insecure configuration of systems. Since no one can possibly know everything about every technology, it is critical that teams see each other's educational pursuits as complimentary. If IT teams focus on vendor-specific certifications, they could provide valuable information to the cybersecurity team. And if cybersecurity teams work on risk management educational pursuits, they can help the IT team prioritize risks instead of trying to fix 300 controls at once.

REFERENCES

Cisco (n.d.). Cisco Certifications. Retrieved from https://www.cisco.com/c/en/us/training-events/training-certifications/certifications.html

CompTIA (n.d.). CompTIA Front Page. Retrieved from https://www.comptia.org/

DoD Cyber Exchange Public (n.d.). DoD approved 8570 baseline certifications. Retrieved from https://public.cyber.mil/cw/cwmp/dod-approved-8570-baseline-certifications/.

EC-Council (n.d.). CEH. Retrieved from https://www.eccouncil.org/programs/certified-ethical-hacker-ceh/

ISC2 (n.d.). (ISC2)2 information security certifications. Retrieved from https://www.isc2.org/Certifications.

Microsoft (n.d.). Microsoft certifications. Retrieved from https://docs.microsoft.com/en-us/learn/certifications/.

Offensive Security (n.d.). Front page. Retrieved from https://www.offensive-security.com/

Chapter 10

Bridging the technology and cybersecurity gap

WHERE WE ARE NOW

Education, training, communication, and collaboration, as well as types of positions and skillsets required in IT and cybersecurity can all lead to contention between teams. Disagreement on its own is not a problem, but prolonged conflict would ultimately lead to unresolved vulnerabilities, unsecure systems, and inability to cooperate on solutions. All these concerns affect risk management, but the *people* aspect is missing from risk management programs. Some typical risks for consideration are vulnerable systems, insecure configurations, insider threats, or physical security. But if teams do not work properly together, applying security settings could take weeks or months, instead of hours or days. This situation is across industries and is not exclusive to one type of IT or cybersecurity team. Organizations must consider how their teams interact as a possible security concern.

IT and cybersecurity teams receive different types of training and education and are focused on competing objectives and goals. With differing skillsets and knowledge of technologies, IT and cybersecurity teams are at odds for either closing tickets or finalizing security assessments. And without executive or management support between teams, even management and executives may have conflicting views for prioritization of projects and budgets. Cybersecurity teams historically receive fewer resources, personnel, and budgets to secure the organization. Even the size of budgets or number of employees available to support security programs affect how much is possible to identify and resolve risks.

With a wide range of challenges in front of IT and cybersecurity teams to collaborate and align goals, how can organizations change their overall security? The first concern is awareness of this issue, even though there are academic researchers who have observed the misaligned goals between IT and cybersecurity teams, are organizations aware of this? What other factors play into a positive interaction of IT and cybersecurity teams and what data is missing in the industry to be able to understand this issue? There are many questions that without awareness of the issue in the industry, or

DOI: 10.1201/9781003264422-10

the willingness to investigate these possible concerns, security programs may never fully mature.

Part of the problem behind complex topics like the eventual insecurity of organizations due to lack of coordination between IT and cybersecurity teams is that it is a difficult conversation to have between management. It could also be challenging to determine if this is a problem within the organization. Initial awareness that IT and cybersecurity teams have conflicting goals, different types of education, and varying levels of technical ability is essential. From awareness, executives and management can have conversations about to help teams collaborate better, fostering an organization of open communication. Even within the IT and cybersecurity teams, awareness lends itself to empathy and understanding for working together to resolve findings, instead of further a contentious relationship.

WHERE WE NEED TO GO

There is quite a bit of work to do to help IT and cybersecurity teams not only work better together but to also improve the security of organizations through these efforts. There is a chain reaction that occurs with even one bad interaction between IT operations and cybersecurity. Even beginning with an email, the security assessment of a system could be delayed, or an audit failed because of this poor interaction. From a delayed assessment could mean more systems are not evaluated because the security assessment team is working to finish the first assessment. More delays increase the time, resources, and financial burden on a project. This increased funding spent on one project could mean that management has to reconsider how many people are on the security team or how many resources provided to that team.

Educational providers for IT and cybersecurity teams need to consider who these teams will collaborate and work with other teams. More technical programs should have courses on communication, emotional intelligence, goal building, and project management. This is not an all-inclusive list, but academic institutions and training programs should provide social sciences and emotional intelligence electives with computer science or cybersecurity courses. Training programs should include modules on human behavior and how technical Subject Matter Expert (SMEs) can interact and communicate effectively with non-technical co-workers.

Ultimately, there is a lot of work to be done across educational, training, communication, and awareness initiatives for IT and cybersecurity personnel. Internal organizational training should identify this as a possible concern and help employees learn how to work well together to achieve the mission and vision of the organization. The industry as a whole should see this as a potential concern and start the conversation with colleagues and consider a communication plan of action between IT and cybersecurity teams. With emotional intelligence, aligning goals, leading with empathy, and integrating IT and cybersecurity liaisons, organizations can achieve cohesion and efficient remediation of security findings.

EMOTIONAL INTELLIGENCE

Emotional intelligence should not be a novel concept for integration and collaboration between IT and cybersecurity teams. Having a high level of emotional intelligence lends an individual to understand, communicate effectively, and comprehend challenges between other teams. There have been many books, articles, webinars, published research, and open discussions about emotional intelligence in leadership, but what about for technical practitioners? Emotional intelligence is taught in academic programs and there are several training providers that offer this subject for individuals in management and leadership positions. But we are missing this critical skill at the practitioner and technical level, with the individuals who are performing the administrative, technical, and security functions.

Emotional intelligence begins with awareness of the subject. Academic institutions, training providers, and certification and accreditation bodies should consider this as a module or component of any IT or cybersecurity course. Currently, IT and cybersecurity personnel learn about all the tools and technology, how to manage and configure them, as well as how to secure them. So why are they not learning effective communication methods to interact with other teams. Security controls are not identified, implemented, and monitored with one person or even one team. These implementation efforts of group policies or secure settings may be done with several IT teams with the aid of cybersecurity groups to verify they are functional and resolve vulnerabilities (Figure 10.1).

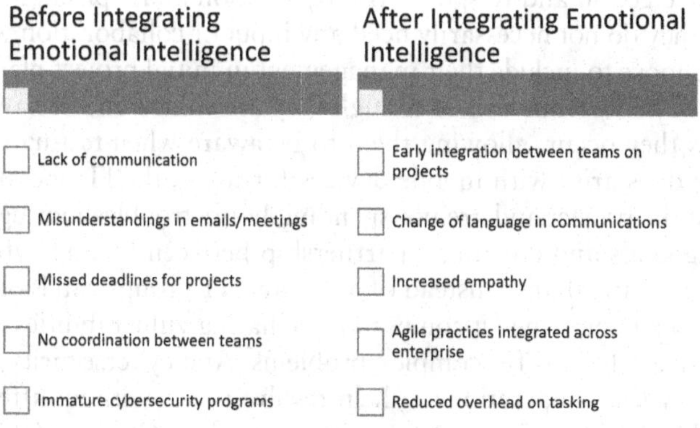

Before Integrating Emotional Intelligence	After Integrating Emotional Intelligence
☐ Lack of communication	☐ Early integration between teams on projects
☐ Misunderstandings in emails/meetings	☐ Change of language in communications
☐ Missed deadlines for projects	☐ Increased empathy
☐ No coordination between teams	☐ Agile practices integrated across enterprise
☐ Immature cybersecurity programs	☐ Reduced overhead on tasking

Figure 10.1 Emotional intelligence: before and after.

Emotional intelligence reaches beyond the ability to understand other teams and communicate effectively; it also encompasses the ability for one to manage and handle our own emotions in a positive way. If team members are easily frustrated, have a difficult time dealing with members from other teams, or are unresponsive to communications with others, courses and awareness of emotional intelligence methods could be incredibly powerful. This is not only a tool to help IT and cybersecurity teams communicate more easily but also to improve one's own skills and lead to further career development. Organizations could also include emotional intelligence, self-awareness, and relationship management courses with their annual cybersecurity training.

ALIGNING GOALS

Improving emotional intelligence throughout IT and cybersecurity groups would have many benefits, one being the understanding of competing goals or priorities. However, in combination with these initiatives, IT and cybersecurity teams could work to align their goals and see where they have tasks and projects in common. There are many projects that may be run in parallel between teams without any awareness from the other teams. This could be a great detriment to the success of said project, but if teams are included from the beginning, there are many benefits. Even if the IT team does not have any need to be involved in a cybersecurity project, the mere act of including them and notifying them of project requirements could display a level of cooperation.

If IT and cybersecurity leadership can communicate openly on ongoing and upcoming projects, there could be alignment for what products are chosen and in what order they are integrated to the environment. From leadership to practitioners, the ability to share projects, tools, and timelines early would possibly identify issues before they affect budget or resources. For example, the cybersecurity team is considering removing the current Endpoint Detection and Response (EDR) solution and replacing with a new product. They do not necessarily need any input or collaboration with the IT team but choose to include their management in initial project planning conversations. The IT team feels as though they are valued and are aware of the changes as they occur, allowing them to be aware when testing is ongoing. If an issue does arise with mobile devices for users, the IT operations team is aware of the project and are not spending hours troubleshooting an issue.

Aligning goals and creating a partnership between IT and cybersecurity groups creates an alliance instead of an enemy. IT groups can look to cybersecurity as a partner when it comes to remediating vulnerabilities and identifying creative solutions for complex problems. And cybersecurity teams can collaborate with IT operations to help resolve issues without affecting user functionality or the business. A Security Operations Center (SOC) can look to IT administrators to answer questions about receiving multiple alerts, and vice versa when a helpdesk is receiving multiple tickets related to an incident. Creating allies between groups increases productivity, improves success rate for projects, and ultimately reduces cost across the business.

LEADING WITH EMPATHY

Leadership is typically talked about in relation to team leads, management, and executive leadership positions. However, leadership is a quality that should be fostered from administrators, analysts, helpdesk technicians, and engineers throughout the organization. Everyone is a leader of their technology, tools, workflows, and customer support engagements. If more technical practitioners were able to see themselves as leaders, they would consider empathy and emotional intelligence as part of their required skills. Leading with empathy is a component of emotional intelligence and is typically taught within those courses. But in a similar fashion, empathy is not commonly taught in vendor-agnostic or vendor-centric certification course, academic institutions, or in training programs.

But empathy is a powerful tool to improve the actual workflow and success of projects in IT and cybersecurity. IT teams who lead with empathy can understand customer requirements, comprehend business strategy, and vision, and collaborate with cybersecurity teams and understand why security assessments are necessary. IT teams without empathy may not spend as much time on customer tickets, delay communications with cybersecurity teams, and ultimately focus on what they believe is important. The same can be said of cybersecurity teams who lead with empathy, they are able to understand the Service Level Agreement (SLA) and functionality requirements of IT operations groups. Cybersecurity teams without empathy would not be willing to compromise or find alternate solutions to vulnerabilities or End of Life (EOL) software. But a cybersecurity team with empathy would help lower risk while aligning with the business strategy.

Empathy should be a requirement, as is the case with emotional intelligence, within any IT or cybersecurity course. There is an ability to add some lessons, case studies, and examples of how situations can occur with and without empathy from team members. Empathy is another 'buzz word' that has been talked about in management and leadership courses, but again, not at the practitioner level. Individuals who are just entering the IT and cybersecurity space are typically focused on technical certifications, undergraduate degrees, and hands-on lab training. But we should consider how soft skills, effective communication, and empathy can impact the bottom line on projects and how teams interact. Organizations can measure the impact of the inclusion of empathy training versus how work has been previously conducted.

Teaching empathy can be done in a variety of ways, from training to open discussions, and even running tabletop exercises. Consider the example from previous sections of a security analyst sending a large vulnerability report to a systems administrator with very little context. If IT operations and cybersecurity team leads and management brought their groups together for open discussion in that exact scenario, it would have them consider the other side of the table when making decisions. It could also encourage greater partnership when it comes to real situations and improve decision-making and critical thinking skills for the practitioner. Open discussion and meeting in an area where groups can share frustrations and ultimately come up with solutions will teach empathy and thereby improve communications between groups.

IT AND SECURITY LIAISONS

IT and cybersecurity teams may have challenging interactions because of their contrasting goals and objectives. Even with the inclusion of empathy and emotional intelligence, there may still be a need for another type of employee within the organization. Liaisons can be a role to work between IT and cybersecurity teams to ensure security and technical pursuits are aligned. For example, an IT liaison could be delegated from the cybersecurity team to collaborate with the operations team on projects and ongoing troubleshooting efforts. A developer liaison could be designated from the cybersecurity team to work on stage gate reviews, security assessments, or providing advice for implementing security controls. A liaison position could either be a portion of a job role, or even better, a specific person hired to work between teams.

An IT liaison from the cybersecurity team would be someone who had an IT operational or engineering background. This individual would have the technical expertise to understand common challenges in those environments, as well as the passion and interest in securing those systems. They would have empathy, understanding, and the interest to solve complex problems and work toward a more cohesive security environment. They would also be effective communicators and be able to align the IT and cybersecurity goals for ongoing projects. This type of position really combines the recommendations from previous sections into one type of role. In smaller teams, the IT liaison may be a delegate from the cybersecurity team who works best with operations groups. In larger organizations, there may be teams of liaisons who collaborate between teams and provide a communication hub to share information throughout teams (Figure 10.2).

A cybersecurity liaison could be a delegate from the IT team who understands security configurations and frameworks. They may not be interested in a full-time position in cyber but may have an attraction to cybersecurity

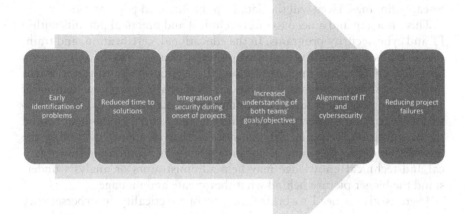

Figure 10.2 Benefits of IT and security liaisons.

and want to learn more. An individual who takes on the role of an inter-mediary may be able to use it as a transition role to move into their desired field. The cybersecurity field is notorious for a difficult barrier to entry, but providing liaison positions is good for candidates interested in cybersecurity, as well as the organization. By working between teams, the individual will build skills in both sectors, meet new teams, and ultimately have opportunities to collaborate on projects. Having liaisons between IT, development, and security teams is beneficial for both the individual and the overall security and operations of an organization.

TECHNICAL AND PRACTICAL MEET

There is this antiquated idea that IT operations groups must be highly technical and not consider other skills like project management, emotional intelligence, or effective communication as essential. This idea of only hiring and retaining highly technical people can compact the issues between IT and cybersecurity teams. If there are only team members who are focused on technology, operations, or management of systems, they are possibly missing the possibilities for expanding and including soft skills. There is terminology in quantitative research used for understanding statistical significance in relation to data analysis. But equally as important with statistical significance is the idea of practical significance. Practical significance is how important findings are to the end user, or the individuals who would be consuming the research findings. How will the data help the intended population?

There is a gap and a need to meet technical and practical pursuits within IT and cybersecurity programs. In the educational, certification, and training methods available for technical pursuits, there is limited information provided on practical implementation. If a systems administrator learns how to install and configure a server OS, do they also learn how that server will be used practically in an environment? For example, would the administrator learn that the servers they build are an essential component behind the organization. Teaching that the systems they create are integral to the business, and how they may be consumed by users. Combining this practical and technical knowledge may help administrators or analysts understand the bigger picture behind what they create and manage.

There is also a need to bridge the gap of practicality in cybersecurity programs. A set of security controls, a framework, or a security assessment does not cover how practical the remediation efforts may be. To understand the practicality of recommendations, cybersecurity professionals should learn how systems operate and are managed by IT teams. If certification or training programs included the implications of what happens when security controls are put in place, there may be more understanding from security practitioners before making recommendations. For example, instead of sending a lengthy report on findings and remediation requirements, a cybersecurity analyst may ask about maintenance windows, help prioritize findings, and help in understanding and implementing the security controls.

CYBERSECURITY FOUNDATIONAL KNOWLEDGE

Cybersecurity foundations are not a typical topic covered in business management, HR, administration, political science, biology, or IT. Throughout academic institutions there are core courses and electives which could be chosen by students as they traverse their desired program. But at this time, almost every industry has gone through a digital transformation and is more reliant on mobile devices. Because cybersecurity and data privacy are top of mind for many home users on their home devices, why is this not a topic covered in academic and certification courses? From HR to business management, cybersecurity affects each layer of an organization and should be a foundational knowledge component of academic and industry training.

While this book is focused on the gaps between IT and cybersecurity, there is a case to include both IT and cybersecurity courses within any profession. The technical gaps between IT and cybersecurity groups are compounded by the lack of training on cybersecurity. If IT groups received cybersecurity training that was focused on why it was important, and not on the security policy of the organization, the teams may have a larger appreciation for each other. Typically, IT users receive cybersecurity training on how to protect privileged accounts and the annual general user cybersecurity training. But what if IT and development teams were taught common digital forensics, incident response, and security analysis job responsibilities during cybersecurity training? Giving a view of what a typical cybersecurity teams tasking, and skillsets are to IT teams can provide an opportunity for increased empathy and understanding.

Cybersecurity should no longer be considered an elective or optional topic for academic, technical, or certification training. It is a critical component for any member of an organization, but increasingly important to understand for IT and development teams. Implementing a cybersecurity first mindset can improve the overall security of an organization and enhance collaboration between teams. For example, consider an IT student takes one or more cybersecurity courses in an undergraduate program. When the student graduates and takes on their first data scientist, helpdesk, or analyst role, they would have a base understanding of cybersecurity requirements for systems. With a built-in expectation of working with a cybersecurity team, there would be fewer concerns about why controls needed to be implemented.

COMMUNICATION GAPS

Communication methods are another missing component of IT and cybersecurity educational programs. IT educational programs cover troubleshooting, critical thinking, programming, and a variety of technical competencies. But communication courses are not necessarily a required component of IT programs and specifically the communication required between IT and cybersecurity teams. The same issue arises in cybersecurity programs that do not teach how to communicate effectively with systems and applications owners. This gap is a critical component to the success of aligning operational and security goals in a practical sense. Educational and training programs need to consider the pragmatic implementation of the skills learned in academic settings and translated to technical professions.

Communication gaps between IT and cybersecurity groups include the method, appropriateness, and timing of interactions. For example, a cybersecurity analyst who is working to finalize an assessment may send an email at the end of the business day. The intention of the analyst is to finish their work for the day so the next day they can start work on their next assessment. However, the IT operations group may receive the email at the end of the day and be frustrated that they were not contacted earlier in the day. They are unable to respond and feel like they need to stay late to review the findings. If the security analyst held the report and sent first thing the next morning, the IT team may be more receptive to the findings. This may seem like a small thing, sending an email at 8 am versus 5 pm the previous night, but the possible impact of that email is far reaching.

When teams collaborate infrequently, or only in highly stressful situations, it can lead to expectations about communication. When IT operations groups only interact with the security team when they are late on remediating vulnerabilities, they may delay communications for security assessments due to concern over negative reactions. And as a chain reaction to this, a security team may be more frustrated and shorter with the IT team because of delayed communications on critical issues. These types of situations continue to compound the gaps between teams and create a severe rift between teams. Whether between a cloud engineer and a security engineer, or between an auditor and systems administrator, these communications could be essential to the security of an infrastructure.

WHERE WE COULD BE

Lack of empathy and understanding, gaps in communication, and lack of integration between technical and practical goals all lead to where we are now. Technical teams who interact with security do not always have a great relationship, ultimately leading to insecure configuration and failed audits. Part of the buildup of these issues is the amount of time that teams have interacted this way, and without the realization that everyday interactions affect security and remediation efforts. But these types of situations and technical gaps do not need to have a negative impact of the security of the environment. Even with awareness of how interactions, communication, and technical and practical skills affect operations and security, there are a number of methods to alleviate these issues and build a more cohesive organization.

IT teams, developers, engineers, and administrators have incredibly stressful jobs, including the uptime and functionality of the systems they manage. They need to adapt to new technology quickly, align technology with the business strategy, and keep users and customers operating according to SLAs. But if computer science, technical training programs, and certification courses had required sections on cybersecurity interaction, more administrators would come into the field with the ability to effectively communicate. If organizations addressed the potential technical and skills gaps between IT and cybersecurity teams with tabletop exercises and open forum discussions, teams would be more cohesive. Instead of having siloed groups with little interaction, systems administrators and security engineers can easily work together and ask questions often, without feeling like a negative interaction is imminent.

Security analysts and engineers also have highly technical and stressful jobs, concerned with the need to secure the environment thoroughly and protect company assets. But individuals in cybersecurity do not always have the IT operations training or understanding of how stressful an operations environment may be. If cybersecurity educational programs contained courses on interactions with system owners and communication methods, there would be more empathy and understanding for inability to remediate vulnerabilities or apply specific controls. Cybersecurity teams should also interface with the entire organization on a regular basis, and not only when performing a security assessment or sending vulnerability reports. If more IT administrators and engineers had regular conversations with cybersecurity teams, communication in stressful situations would have less tension.

The opportunities are available to improve communication, teamwork, and the overall security of an organization. With awareness, integration of these ideals into training and academic programs, and the willingness to collaborate, IT and cybersecurity teams can bridge technical and skills gaps. Technical and skills gaps between IT and cybersecurity teams do not negatively impact an organization. Teams are trained differently to meet different functions, and when IT and cybersecurity teams collaborate well, they complement each other's skills. When IT teams provide the technical limitations or constraints on a system, and the cybersecurity team can come up with mitigating controls for a known risk, organizations are able to enable to align business strategy and security goals.

Chapter 11

Embracing functionality and security

MISSED OPPORTUNITIES

The heart of the problem, the technical gaps between IT and cybersecurity teams, stems from several missed opportunities within organizations. These opportunities arise from interactions between teams, education and training opportunities, and even corporate policies. Consider a security policy outlined by the organization that does not provide technical instruction and is vague on the implementation of what security framework or level of security must be achieved. This would provide very little information to systems owners, and when the first security assessment or vulnerability report is handed to them, they may be blindsided with the information. Even if the team is running their own vulnerability scans and reviewing results, they may not understand the need to remediate vulnerabilities scored as Medium (by the Common Vulnerability Scoring System (CVSS)) within a certain window.

There are also missed opportunities outside of organizations, but within the training, certification, and academic opportunities provided to IT and cybersecurity students. There is an incredible need to provide courses not just on effective communication, but on effective communication between teams. Any IT professional could benefit from the early awareness that they would need to collaborate with cybersecurity teams within undergraduate and entry-level certification programs. Similarly, cybersecurity groups would benefit from a required course on IT operations requirements and SLAs. It is critical to teach cyber professionals about the integration of cybersecurity into operations teams, instead of solely the application of controls and secure configurations of systems.

Another potential opportunity for IT and cybersecurity professionals is teaching adaptability and flexibility. This aligns with the need to train critical thinking and problem-solving skills. Individuals across technical teams must be adaptable and consider alternative options. With the increased complexity of systems and environments, reliance on End of Life (EOL) applications, and widespread usage of open-source software, IT and cybersecurity professionals must adapt. It is not possible to continue to build applications on EOL systems, but on the same side, it is impossible to apply

DOI: 10.1201/9781003264422-11

all security controls to reach 100% locked-down systems. There must be creativity, innovation, and adaptability to implement security controls and balance the functionality and operability of users.

Missed opportunities across communication, technology, and collaboration between teams impact several areas of the business. One of these opportunities is the overload of tools and software integrated into IT and security teams. There was a great push to build and purchase more tools and technology to identify security issues, monitor systems, and troubleshoot common issues. But the number of tools in any team increases the complexity, management, and overhead administration for technical professionals. More tools mean more patching, security controls, configuration, and re-configuration to meet changing business needs. In a similar fashion, uprooting current tooling and replacing with new tools is not always the best solution, and sometimes comes at a cost for revenue, budgets, and resource management. If teams are constantly removing and implementing new software and devices, there is limited time for innovation or reconfiguring systems for optimal use and coverage.

FUNCTIONALITY IS NOT A FOUR-LETTER WORD

IT operations teams are aware of the need for constant functionality for users. A stable environment is one of the basic requirements of an IT team, and they must manage production systems while integrating new technology and improvements. Functionality and operability are the 'bread and butter' for IT operations teams, and any security requirements are a secondary request from their daily activities. This may be a frustration for security teams who are focused on the potential risks of unmitigated vulnerabilities across systems. Security teams, as mentioned previously, focus on security first and functionality as a secondary aspect of systems. These competing priorities often lead to frustration and concern from the security team if findings are not remediated in a short time.

But why is functionality not a main concern for security personnel? Consider a situation where security teams are met with a challenging condition, for example, an IT team that cannot upgrade systems because of customer functionality. The security team is told that the systems cannot be upgraded to the latest version because of potential downtime, degraded user service, and other concerns with functionality. Security analysts receive notice from management that they will need exemptions for these applications and will not be fixing them any time soon. Even though the team is disappointed, this does not have to be the end of the conversation.

When a security team can come to an IT group in this situation and provide a technical solution for the inability to upgrade, the conversation may change among the administrators and management. For example, the security team could propose a 3-month upgrade that would include the creation of new cloud servers, installation of the updated application, and a migration plan for users with a pilot program and ultimately move to production and the decommission of old systems. This outline shows the IT team the willingness for security to help provide long-term solutions to resolve security findings, while also being understanding of customer and business requirements. If the security team can show the technical upgrade path, it may also go a long way to improve the relationship between teams. IT teams may not assume that security professionals are highly technical, and depending on what their past interactions have been, they may not have had the ability to demonstrate those skills.

When the security team embraces functionality for IT systems, they can resolve a multitude of security findings. Even if the vulnerabilities or risks are not resolved overnight, there may be a clear path forward to decommission and remove EOL systems. One of the biggest hurdles for security teams are waivers or exemptions listed for critical and exploitable vulnerabilities. If there is more consideration for the current infrastructure and what needs to be put in place to resolve the findings, IT and cybersecurity teams may collaborate more easily. Creating a master plan to resolve waivers and exemptions will also possibly provide increased functionality for users. New technology can resolve vulnerabilities and resolve bugs or issues that users may note in the older applications. EOL applications and devices can be an opportunity to increase user functionality, instead of negatively impact it.

EMBRACING SECURITY

On the other side of the functionality coin sits the ability for IT teams and management to embrace security. There is a history of security teams being the 'Office of No', where risk management is done by remediating all findings, implementing all the security controls, and saying no when it came to new products and solutions. But this is not the true spirit of security, nor is it how security teams operate in current environments. IT teams may have had poor interactions, frustrating experiences, and tumultuous relationships with security teams. There is a need for operations, development, and engineering teams to reconsider relationships with security teams and how it impacts their systems.

A new perspective on security could be taught to students, through training, or even through interaction with the cybersecurity analysts and engineers that work for the organization. If IT teams were able to see how security controls not only protect the systems they manage but also can keep users and data safe, it may alter their perception. For example, if a developer was able to work with a security engineer at the onset and throughout the project, their relationship and perspective of security may change. Instead of seeing security personnel at the end of the project and bringing up a variety of vulnerabilities and delaying the production date, they would see security personnel at the onset. The project is on time, security is involved and actively providing solutions, and the application goes to production with minimal changes.

Embracing security in this situation encourages new ways of thinking and changing the way teams collaborate. Security can be encouraged in other projects and tasks as well and can be encouraged from management down to technical professionals. When executive and upper-level management support and embrace security objectives in combination with IT and business strategy, the teams would work more cohesively. This support leads to lowering pilot to production time, increasing overall security of systems, and time for innovation between teams. IT and security teams have complementary skills, and if they partner on more projects, they may find more innovation in projects and tools.

PROBLEM-SOLVING AND DECISION-MAKING

There are a great many books, articles, and research on the power of problem-solving and decision-making for management and leadership. There are also many programs that include some aspect of problem-solving within technical academic and training institutions. But how can problem-solving and decision-making methods alter the way that IT and cybersecurity teams communicate and collaborate on projects. Like aligning goals or communicating more effectively, IT and cybersecurity teams consider problem-solving and decision-making for projects in completely different ways. But these differences can be seen as strengths, instead of weaknesses, for meeting technical and security goals.

IT engineers and developers are very logical in decision-making when it comes to what tools to use, how to solve complex problems, and how to handle outages and functionality concerns. Engineers take time to logically consider impacts of changes on the system, any interdependencies with other applications, and how users might be affected by the changes. For example, a group of users are unable to access an application, while most other users are able to log in and use the application successfully. The engineers would first investigate permissions issues, any systems that may be unreachable or down, and many other scenarios. They may also review change logs to see what changes were made in the application last and if those impacted users. Decisions on how to resolve the issue would be based on potential risk to users versus potentially improving the situation for the users affected.

Cybersecurity analysts and engineers make decisions more based on the risk to the organization. For example, if an alert for malware is noted on a system, the analyst may make the decision to contain the machine even if it impacts user functionality. The decision to contain the machine instead of continuing to monitor could be based on a variety of factors; a user with administrative permissions, sensitivity of data on the system, or possibility for an attacker to gain a foothold and leverage that system to gain access to application servers. Decisions may also be based on the overall risk to the infrastructure and the need to protect the entire environment versus one users' functionality. This is quite different from how IT teams would make decisions since cybersecurity is more concerned with the long-term risk to users versus a current outage or issue.

Even though each team solves problems in different ways, they can be complimentary and when working together, could identify and resolve issues quickly. For example, consider the example of containing a machine when malware or malicious files are detected. If there is open communication between the helpdesk and the Security Operations Center (SOC), when the machine is contained the SOC would notify the helpdesk and the user at the same time. This would provide understanding to the user for why they are no longer able to access applications, as well as proactively stop any tickets from going to the helpdesk.

ENCOURAGING BOTH OPERATIONS AND CYBERSECURITY

The relationships between IT operations, development, and security teams should be evaluated by higher level management to determine if this phenomenon exists in the organization. It is certainly possible that the teams already coexist and function well together, but if this is not the case, the leadership teams of both groups need to collaborate. When management leads the discussion and encourages partnership between practitioners, they can teach by designing programs around the partnership. For example, when the CIO and CISO meet regularly, partner in communications, and interact with the IT and security teams, they show a need for this type of behavior throughout the organization.

If the executive and senior leadership of the IT and security teams meet regularly, they could pull in practitioners from both teams and start the partnership by observation. When the technical team members see open discussion and communication between the Chief Information Officer (CIO) and Chief Information Security Officer (CISO) offices, they utilize those same principles within their teams. Consider an organization where the CIO and CISO regularly encourage meetings between the groups, both social and for technical projects. Even in an environment where there is long-standing tension, there is always room for the executive team to step in and encourage collaboration and move the technology, processes, and *people* in a positive direction.

Without the encouragement from executive management, projects fail, applications will continue to run on EOL software and unsupported systems, and the maturity of the IT and cybersecurity programs will stall. A maturity model can be created to integrate the teams' projects, for example, in an organization that is working on developing a new product. The development team has already started the project and have not met with the security team or considered how vulnerabilities and misconfigurations may affect the product. Management could start with an introductory meeting so that the development and security teams can interact and demonstrate their technical expertise. Then the leadership could set up regular calls between the groups and provide support for both sets of objectives. While a partnership will not happen overnight, the increased collaboration on this project will lead to better interactions on future projects.

COMPROMISE AS A TOOL

Personal and professional relationships can benefit by using compromise in delicate situations. Compromise means that each team would work toward an agreement on the tools, technology, and security measures to put in place. This does not mean that each team achieves every item on their list during a project but would be able to come up with creative solutions. IT and cybersecurity teams have differing and sometimes competing goals in projects, but compromise could lead to a stable and secure environment. For example, a security team that is working on a security assessment for a system containing EOL software. They come up with a plan to provide mitigating controls as short-term goals and are able to provide a vision for long-term security. This compromise means that the project can continue moving forward, while not allowing the systems to remain on unsupported systems.

Another example would be an IT team that has been working on upgrading email systems for the organization. The engineers have been working on this solution for several months and are concerned that the security team is getting involved after the project timeline and technical upgrade have already begun. Management encourages the teams to come up with a solution that would remediate some vulnerabilities, with a timeline to remediate the other findings that can keep the project on schedule. The security team works up a list that will provide which items to resolve first, dependencies on other technology in the environment, as well as offering support to the technical team. The security team knows that not every finding will be remediated immediately, and compromises to come up with a more long-term solution.

From the cybersecurity perspective, consider a group of security assessors/auditors that have performed a security assessment on several databases. They have found several critical vulnerabilities, missing security controls, and physical hardware using older OS levels that are unsupported by the vendor. The security team is initially frustrated that this system has been running without proper controls in place. But instead of providing a report and failing the team for the assessment, they offer mitigating controls and an upgrade path to the administrators. They are able to hold the technical team accountable for the security findings, while also providing support and understanding that the systems could not be brought down overnight to fix the incredible number of issues. This compromise will ultimately lead to the upgrade of those systems, instead of increasing tension and frustration between the teams.

ADAPTABILITY

Compromise over security findings leads to the adaptability and flexibility of IT and cybersecurity teams. Technology, security frameworks, policies, and guidelines change constantly, and teams must be willing to adapt to these changes. While it can be a lot of information for practitioners to adapt to, it is increasingly beneficial to adapt to those changes. Without the willingness to change directions on a project, teams may stagnate and would ultimately lead to disgruntled and frustrated employees. For example, consider a helpdesk technician who is constantly working with customers, while trying to keep up with ongoing IT projects, system maintenance and upgrades, as well as changing policies in the organization. Without the willingness to change processes, the technician may have difficulty closing customer tickets, working with customers on functionality issues, and ultimately working with higher level engineers.

Another example of adaptability is from the security practitioners in an SOC. An SOC is a place of constant alerts, reviewing network traffic, as well as monitoring for changes in the environment. Types of attacks and exploits change every day and sometimes multiple times a day. Security policies, requirements from management, and technical projects are also just as fluid. Without flexibility in their potential duties for the day, a security analyst may miss alerts or misconfiguration settings on a system in vulnerability reports. Because the cybersecurity field, in general, is changing so rapidly, security team members must be adaptable to changing technology, increasingly complex vulnerabilities, and how new frameworks may be integrated into security programs. But adaptability is not just for the technology and processes used within the team and organization.

Adaptability is also in the daily interactions of IT and cybersecurity teams. For example, in a large-scale event like SolarWinds or Log4Shell, teams must understand that information changes very quickly. It is easy to be frustrated when the IT or development teams have spent hours working on remediation activities, only to find out that there is new information on the exploit. Cybersecurity teams try to provide the most up-to-date and accurate findings available on an exploit, but in major incidents it can be difficult to have all the data upfront. For example, a vendor will release as much information as they can provide that is accurate. This means that the teams must adapt to changing circumstances, for example, what level to patch a system to, and even how many patches are available at the time of disclosure.

UNDERSTANDING COGNITIVE LIMITATIONS

Team cohesion, adaptability, and compromise are all important for improving relationships and ultimately the security of an organization. But one of the factors that influences the maturity level and success of a security program is the understanding of psychological factors on technical professionals. There is a lot of research and current literature that point to the missing link in IT and cybersecurity: the human factors. The *technology* and functionality are available to support our operations teams, and organizations can implement supporting *processes* and policies, but understanding how the *people* of our organization affect security programs is lacking. While these psychology principles apply to users as well, the focus is understanding how these concepts impact our IT and cybersecurity teams.

Every organization has some level of security awareness programs aimed at helping users understand the importance of security. But one of the gaps in security training is how IT and cybersecurity personnel understand and utilize security standards. Educational levels, common skills, and team goals do not cover the psychological and behavioral traits of technical professionals. One very important element to discuss is how cognitive limitations affect IT and cybersecurity teams. Cognitive limitations can be caused by information overload, perceptions and biases, or the need to act quickly in stressful situations (Andrade and Yoo, 2019). Any of these items can lead practitioners to make poor decisions and impact project status, security objectives, and user functionality.

For example, consider an SOC analyst who must manage three different Endpoint Detection and Response (EDR), antivirus, and anti-malware consoles during the day, along with various network and vulnerability monitoring scans and real-time dashboards. For an entire workday, every day, the analyst must review alerts and act on any that seem potentially malicious and investigate them further. This is an incredible amount of information given to an individual and they must act quickly on alerts that could negatively impact the environment. It is possible that based on the various consoles and dashboards they review, plus false-positive alerts, they may lose focus and either miss alerts or be overwhelmed with the amount of information to ingest (Figure 11.1).

This is only one example of how cognitive limitations could impact decision-making for IT or cybersecurity professionals. Consider the compounded cognitive limitations for teams based on the constant input of

Figure 11.1 Amount of information going to an SOC analyst.

information from monitoring systems, media, technical training, research, projects management, and ongoing tasking. As IT infrastructure becomes more complex and leans to hybrid cloud models, there are more systems to manage for administrators, and even more security settings to consider for security analysts and engineers. Management and practitioners should consider how cognitive limitations may impact themselves and others within their teams. Understanding this phenomenon can help them empathize with teammates and other groups within the organization.

UNDERSTANDING PERSONALITY TYPES

Cognitive limitations are one component for individuals and management to consider in IT and cybersecurity programs, but several other psychological concepts could be integrated into the organization. Behavioral analysis techniques may be used by insider threat programs to identify malicious insiders. But these techniques are applicable to other groups within the organization and can be used to help teams empathize with each other. Behavioral analysis is the study of understanding human behavior with the intention to change or alter bad behaviors, for example, helping someone to understand why they bite their nails and help encourage them to stop

(Lahcen et al., 2020). There are many techniques used by behavioral analysts, but of particular interest is identifying and understanding personality types of technical practitioners.

For example, a systems administrator who is more introverted and prefers to work along on projects. This individual does not mind working in a team setting but works more efficiently on tasks sitting in their office with the door closed. This may come across as standoffish or someone who is difficult to work with if the security team is not aware of this personality trait. The security team has had very little interaction with the administrator, which has led to increased time spent on the security assessment. The security team is frustrated and complains to management about the lack of communication from the IT administrator. The IT and security team leads meet to discuss the concerns and ultimately leave the meetings with increased tension and no resolution (Figure 11.2).

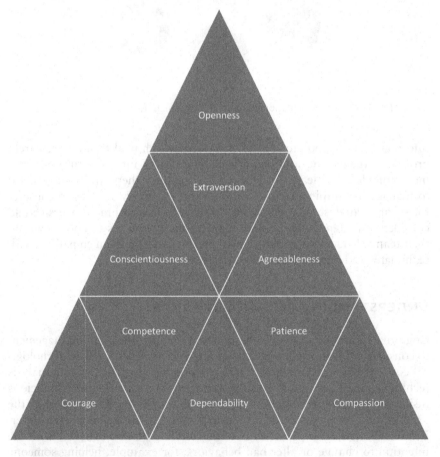

Figure 11.2 **Personality types.**

A situation like this would have been quite different if, when the team leads met, they discussed that there may need to be a new meeting with the security lead and administrator to understand the best communication methods. The IT administrator may prefer email and direct messages versus constantly meeting to discuss findings. If the team leads came together and agreed to handle this situation differently, it is possible that the administrator would respond quickly to emails and resolve findings within the agreed upon timeline. With understanding and adapting to someone's preferred communication methods, findings can be remediated and ultimately improve the interactions between the teams. It is more likely that the IT administrator would be appreciative of the flexibility and willingness to work around their preferred contact methods. People, in general, are much more agreeable and will collaborate when accommodations are made to meet their personality and preferences.

OUR DIFFERENCES MAKE OUR TEAMS STRONGER

There seems to be a pattern of frustration between teams, concerns over other teams' skillsets, and lack of trust between IT and cybersecurity teams. Whether the mistrust stems from previous interactions or contention over education and technical skills, it compounds the issues over time. Instead of the IT team believing that the cybersecurity team does not have the same depth of technical knowledge, what if they saw them as an ally to fill in the gaps in their security knowledge? There is an incredible need for IT and cybersecurity teams to collaborate and reconsider how they interact with each other. There is not a skills gap or a technical gap, but a lack of understanding and inability to see each other's skills as strengths, not weaknesses.

A software developer may have very deep knowledge of C++ and Javascript, as well as the ability to create programs quickly and learn new programming languages to meet customer needs. However, they were not trained in secure development practices and do not typically build code securely at the onset of the project. When a security engineer joins the project to assist on vulnerability scans and code reviews, the developer is initially frustrated and concerned that they want them to address so many vulnerabilities. However, what if the perspective of the developer evolved from an anger around lack of development knowledge to the understanding that their security skillset complements their programming competences. This shift in perspective would change the perception of their interactions from negative to positive and increase the trust of the findings from the security analyst.

While there has been mistrust and lack of willingness to work together in the past, IT and cybersecurity teams are incredibly complementary groups. If executive management and team leadership can see these differences as assets, their teamwork, security of the network, and functionality of the environment will only improve. The combination of increased communication, willingness to adapt and learn, and understanding of psychological and human behaviors will create well-rounded teams. There are so many opportunities to change the way teams interact, mostly with awareness and willingness to adapt to how people work at their best. But this adaptability must come from both teams and must be consistent, or else these tactics will be short-lived and not change the overall negative behavior. Positive behavior change takes time and the commitment to evolving the way teams work together.

REFERENCES

Andrade, R. O., & Yoo, S. G. (2019). Cognitive security: A comprehensive study of cognitive science in cybersecurity. *Journal of Information Security and Applications*, 48. doi:10.1016/j.jisa.2019.06.008.

Lahcen, R. A. M., Caulkins, B., Mohapatra, R., & Kumar, M. (2020). Review and insight on the behavioral aspects of cybersecurity. *Cybersecurity*, 3(1), 1–8.

Chapter 12

Creating new roles

THINKING OUTSIDE CURRENT JOB DESCRIPTIONS

If practitioners, teams, and management can start thinking about the implications of communications, technical skills gaps, and job responsibilities a bit differently, this could considerably impact the security of the organization. Job descriptions are sometimes quite long, filled with required certifications and education, and a long list of required duties. However, there are very rarely any indications of the teams that the individual would have to interact with. For example, a systems administrator position may list required programming languages, systems, and technology to manage, as well as a required bachelor's degree. But how do any of these skills translate into effective communication, teamwork, and collaboration between the Security Operations Center (SOC) and any security assessors/auditors that may assess those systems.

When an individual gets through the initial resume process and into an interview, they may have a technical skills challenge or several interviews with management and team members. These interviews may challenge their technical knowledge and see how they would fit within the team. But do the interviews include a section on cybersecurity knowledge or how the teams would collaborate on projects and tasking? The questions that the interviewee is asked to pertain more to their knowledge and skillset, and even how they would handle situations when on the job. But this leaves out a potentially critical area of securing systems. The administrator may need to have a basic understanding of security controls and how to run vulnerability scans. But this does not cover the actual ongoing collaboration and communication required to work with the security team.

What if hiring managers for IT and cybersecurity programs collaborated on job postings? They could share what a typical day looks like for the practitioners and maybe look for personnel who are willing to collaborate and communicate between the teams. For example, a cybersecurity team hires an analyst who is interested in being a cloud engineer. They would be able to hire them on the cybersecurity team and eventually move them over to the infrastructure team, which creates an ally between both teams. If the

DOI: 10.1201/9781003264422-12

IT team hired a systems administrator who was interested in working at an SOC, both teams benefit from having someone who has interests in both areas. Hiring individuals like this with interests in both IT and cybersecurity solve several the hiring challenges in today's market. Potential hires are given a career path, an openness between teams to move people around, which increases retention and growth in skillsets.

NEW TYPES OF IT ROLES

It was incredibly common to have IT generalists several years ago, but more organizations are hiring for IT specialists, or someone who has a specialty in a specific technology. For example, cloud engineer job descriptions may speak to one type of cloud technology. Or a developer position may be looking for someone to work on one type of language for one product. Whether IT specialist or IT generalists, there is room for improvement on current IT job roles and descriptions. The market needs multidimensional and innovative individuals to enhance IT teams and not just manage systems but troubleshoot complex issues and ultimately improve the systems they manage. What if IT job descriptions included career pathing, communication and relationships with other teams, and better terminology to describe the position.

For example, instead of a systems engineer, a systems collaboration engineer, or a systems innovation engineer. These additional terms may encourage different types of candidates to apply and show to the applicant that the systems engineering position is more than management and operations. There could also be a role for systems security engineering that would combine the efforts of management and securing the systems they are responsible for. Engineers would be encouraged to have some security knowledge and the job description could point to the necessary collaboration between teams. Encouraging a partnership from as early as the job description would help remove the negative perception from IT to security teams. A systems security engineer could also be interested in a career in cybersecurity but is still working on the IT side.

Other roles to consider in IT are upgrade specialists, End of Life (EOL) migration specialists, or systems development engineers. Consider the lifecycle of systems and how someone may be able to bring value to the team by specializing in complicated upgrades. Many organizations are stuck on legacy equipment or applications, hiring someone who specializes in upgrades can improve the functionality and security of an IT group without specifically requiring cybersecurity experience. There are several ways a migration specialist could be beneficial to the IT team, from removing EOL upgrades to moving on-premises systems to the cloud. Consider how job descriptions can point to realistic expectations, and not use generic terminology, which may attract a more diverse candidate pool.

NEW TYPES OF CYBERSECURITY ROLES

Similarly in the cybersecurity field, there is a need for security positions that consider the interactions and relationships that need to be formed between groups. Cybersecurity job descriptions are typically focused on the required security frameworks, certifications, and education, and the tasking associated with SOC alert monitoring, security assessment requirements, or documentation creation. Security engineers and architects are focused on the integration of security practices into the infrastructure or as part of the application development process. But there are many other areas of expertise within the cybersecurity domain, including innovation, operations, and development.

For example, cybersecurity professionals must understand frameworks, guidelines, business policy, and multiple layers of the organization. Instead of job titles and descriptions like security engineer or architect, what about security policy developer or secure U/X designer. Integrating security into a job role like design and policy creation allow for 'secure by design' principles within the organization. Job descriptions that include terminology like these help the applicant to understand a bit more of the specifics and provide a specialization for individuals with multiple interests. Instead of focusing solely on security engineering, they could focus on human factors security engineering or Java secure engineering. These types of job roles also expand the skillsets and niches that cybersecurity professionals may be looking for in career development.

Typical job roles and descriptions can be incredibly generic and not really address the overall requirements and desired skillsets. Instead, consider IT and security implications within the job descriptions as well. For example, consider an SOC analyst position that would need to monitor and review alerts by multiple tools. The SOC analyst job description could also the collaboration with IT operations groups, ability to attend meetings and learn from security engineers, as well as project tasking for vulnerability remediation efforts. This changes the job description from required or desired skills to the ability for the analyst to learn and grow within the role. This enhanced description can ultimately lead to improved retention, upskilling analysts who may move up to engineers and analysts within the organization (Figure 12.1).

IT SECURITY LIAISON

As mentioned previously, there are many opportunities to create a specialization in the workforce for IT and cybersecurity collaboration and partnership. One such idea for job roles are IT or security liaisons. Individuals would work between operations, development, engineering, and cybersecurity teams to build a partnership. The job roles may vary depending on the

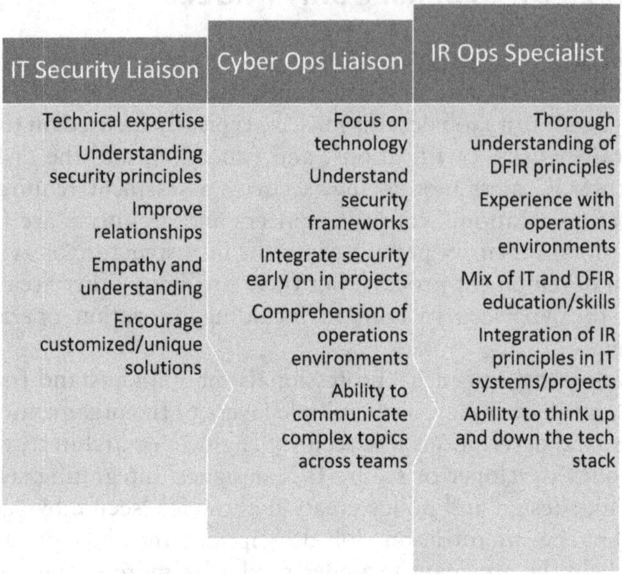

IT Security Liaison	Cyber Ops Liaison	IR Ops Specialist
Technical expertise	Focus on technology	Thorough understanding of DFIR principles
Understanding security principles	Understand security frameworks	Experience with operations environments
Improve relationships	Integrate security early on in projects	Mix of IT and DFIR education/skills
Empathy and understanding	Comprehension of operations environments	Integration of IR principles in IT systems/projects
Encourage customized/unique solutions	Ability to communicate complex topics across teams	Ability to think up and down the tech stack

Figure 12.1 New types of IT and cyber roles and descriptions.

size of the organization, but the goal would be to improve relationships, bring security into projects early, and integrate security into DevOps programs. Even with the idea of DevSecOps, or the integration of development, security, and operations groups, there is still a need to encourage this idea early on in projects.

Consider a job role for a security engineering liaison, someone who has a background in both cybersecurity and software development, with a knack for communication and empathy. An IT security liaison would be in a similar role who would help coordinate efforts between the IT operations and security groups. They would be able to run and understand vulnerability reports, be aware of maintenance windows and current IT projects, as well as have a highly technical background and understanding of security principles. This individual would be skilled in effective communication, willing to work with multiple teams, and interested in engaging in both IT and cybersecurity projects.

This role could be incredibly powerful as an ally to both IT and cybersecurity teams. Supporting both groups, they could help with the flow of communication, as well as ease any tensions that may arise from competing goals or projects. They may also be integral in identifying and resolving problems quickly. For example, consider an IT project that is installing a product that is known to have multiple vulnerabilities. The IT security liaison may be aware of these security concerns and notify the IT group before they decide to use that product. This early warning would let the IT team know that they may need to consider other options, and the liaison could help them find an alternative product.

CYBERSECURITY OPERATIONS LIAISON

A cybersecurity operations liaison would fulfill a complementary role to an IT security liaison. The same skillsets of someone who can understand multiple forms of technology up and down the stack would be essential for this role. This position would incorporate knowledge of operations environments in IT or development teams, incorporating their cybersecurity and communication skills. The liaison would sit between the SOC and the systems owners, working between the teams when there are minor incidents or helping to identify major incidents early on. Having a liaison who understands the demands and time constraints behind an operations environment would be incredibly beneficial for coordinating incidents and reviewing alerts.

Systems owners would have a trusted contact on the SOC that they could coordinate with for security concerns and alerts. The cybersecurity operations liaison would also provide support for technical Points of Contact who may need to be notified in the event of an incident. This type of position increases the communication to the right personnel in the event of an incident or a suspected incident. In any IR program, the time from identification, notification, or containment are critical when dealing with ransomware or fast-moving malware. But this liaison would do more than notify systems owners or assist the SOC, and they could also be a trusted resource for systems owners.

For example, when systems owners are working through security assessments or understanding what kind of risks exist in their environment, they may turn to the liaison. The cybersecurity operations liaison would have access and knowledge about risk management and provide guidance on what to remediate first. These liaison positions allow individuals to step one foot into operations while having the other foot in risk management and problem-solving at different levels. Positions like this, again, allow for personal and professional growth, and allow individuals with multiple interests to pursue them all within one role.

INCIDENT RESPONSE/OPERATIONS SPECIALIST

Typical positions in an IR group are prepared to handle an incident following a methodological process. Incidents are contained to one or a group of systems, or if that is not possible, will work to identify how the malicious actors accessed the environment. The team will identify entry point and collect associated logs and network traffic, along with a host of other tasks to track the incident. But what if IR teams also contained operations specialists who understood the SLAs and typical uptime for systems on the network. In larger environments, there could be multiple applications and services that cannot be disrupted or may need notice before taking systems down.

Even with the wide range of skills on an IR team, having an operations specialist may help them when it comes to decisions for containing versus investigating machines. For example, consider an environment with three major applications that are used by customers and require an uptime of 99% per the SLA. An IR operations specialist would understand the requirements of those systems and be able to provide the best advice to manage risk while still supporting customers. They may also be able to provide advice for application owners on building resiliency into their systems before an incident occurs. An IR operations specialist may be able to work on either a development or IR team and provide context in the event of an incident.

A unique position like this enables an incredible number of aspects of the business. From understanding the application and customer support requirements, to how to best handle IR activities within the organization. Having multidimensional job positions can really increase the maturity of the projects and programs involved. If an IR operations specialist works directly on the IR team, with a background in IT operations they may help the team consider alternatives they were not aware of. And if they were placed on an application development team, they could help that team understand resiliency and what it means to be involved in an incident. Each team learns new skills, enhances their security and operating procedures, and ultimately creates a culture of collaboration.

IT/CYBERSECURITY COOPERATION WORKING GROUP

Even if a hybrid job role like IR operations specialist or cybersecurity operations liaison officer would not work with an organization, a working group may fill that gap. Consider an IT/Cybersecurity cooperation group, where a delegate from different IT and cybersecurity teams can come together once a month or once a quarter and discuss their work. Having a regular interaction between teams can provide a standardized format for sharing projects, tasking, and any concerns in technical or security controls. When engaging on new projects, IT and cybersecurity teams would connect during the working group sessions to discuss best products, most secure options, and how the teams can coordinate project tasks.

Working groups can go beyond project tasks and discussing security assessments, but to how to resolve ongoing issues and mature both programs.

One of the ongoing issues between both IT and cybersecurity teams is the backlog of issues and security risks, while trying to balance operations and integration of new tools and applications. If the teams can come together on a regular basis and work through the backlog of issues, they can focus more time on innovation and upskilling team members. For example, if there is a backlog of 50 vulnerabilities that need to be resolved, these working groups can focus on these initially, and once resolved they can start working on other projects. These projects could be consolidating security tools, resolving lower severity vulnerabilities, or even working on improving the overall security architecture and design.

These working groups can also have a social or networking component for both IT and cybersecurity professionals. Making connections between teams could lead to job opportunities that would keep skilled individuals within the organization. Having members move between teams could create even more cohesion and collaboration. For example, an administrator from the IT operations group who works well with the SOC analysts wants to consider a position within the SOC. Since the team is already aware of this individual, have worked on projects before, and have had a positive impact on security projects, they are welcomed to the team. The SOC gains an analyst who is excited about security and has a great understanding of the IT infrastructure, and the IT operations team gains an ally on the SOC. This situation is a great benefit to both teams, and the overall security posture of the organization.

HUMAN FACTORS SECURITY ENGINEER

Human factors engineering is the combination of psychology, engineering, and design concepts to build more effective tools for users and consumers of technology. Human factors work is most classically seen in technology within User Experience (UX) and design groups, working to enhance applications and tools User Interface. Specifically human factors incorporate the understanding of how users work with tools and developing and enhancing interfaces to improve productivity. Human factors security research goes back as far as the early 2000s, but there has been little integration of these two fields within small and large organizations.

A role like a Human Factors Security Engineer (HFSE) would be a major benefit to SOCs, IR teams, blue team and network defense groups, as well as security assessment teams. An HFSE would focus on the integration of psychological and engineering principles which complement the cybersecurity field. For example, this individual would work with the SOC to understand what tools they manage, dashboards they use, and other applications that they use to conduct daily tasking and manage alerts. The HFSE may be able to provide consolidated dashboards, enhance the alerting to remove false-positive alerts, and automate manual processes for the SOC analysts. This allows the analyst to review fewer unrelated alerts and focus on potentially malicious events and identify incidents more quickly.

An HFSE position could positively impact blue teams and network defenders as well. With the knowledge of security principles with the combination of how users interact with systems, they may help to identify possible entry points for malicious attackers. An HFSE would also be able to assist with Insider Threat groups and provide guidance for malicious insiders and associated behavior. This position, like a cybersecurity operations specialist, would be able to work between multiple cybersecurity groups and help the collaboration in larger cyber groups. If there are many security groups throughout the organization, someone in this role could serve as a delegate or liaison to improve communication on projects and risk management activities.

Someone with a background in human factors and works on a cybersecurity team would also be an integral part of the UX/design team. They could help to provide security configuration or alerting within applications, as well as offer advice for improving design to enhance visibility of secure configuration. Design teams conduct user enhancement testing and focus groups to understand user challenges or functionality requirements. The HFSE could integrate into design projects to show how to easily display security information to users. This encourages a 'shift left' mindset for security and adds awareness of security information while users interact with applications, and not only once a year during security awareness training.

HUMAN FACTORS IT SPECIALIST

Along similar lines, human factors can be a positive benefit to IT teams, whether in operations or development groups. A Human Factors IT Specialist (HFIS) would have a technical background with education or experience in human factors and design. They may have an undergraduate degree in user design or have worked in an IT operations group and moved to a UX or design team. With a background in IT operations and an interest in design, they could provide incredible support to either side of the organizations. Whether the HFIS works on the IT or design side, they would be an ally between both teams and could give insight on projects and tasking.

An HFIS professional would prioritize functionality and uptime, while also be concerned with how users understand and utilize the technology available to them. For example, consider a virtual desktop environment that is managed by a remote access team with administrators and engineers. They recently have had issues with slow logon times and user functionality issues and are unable to figure out technically why users are having issues. The team hires an HFIS to evaluate how the users interact with the virtual desktops and find that it is not a technical issue, but a design flaw in how the users see the desktops within the web application. With a design change on

Figure 12.2 Integrating HFE into cybersecurity.

the web application view, users can see the desktops easier and are able to log in without issue (Figure 12.2).

On the design side, an HFIS professional could provide expertise in how operations teams function and how that affects the design of products. For example, a design team is trying to enhance the workflow of a web application so users can submit forms for approval easier. While this design is easier for users, it requires changes on the backend with application upgrades that must be done during the maintenance window. With the operations and technical knowledge, the HFIS collaborates between the operations group and helps the design team schedule the changes. This partnership introduces the operations team to the designers, and they learn the regular maintenance windows and plan design changes accordingly. Each team gets an ally, coordinates more efficiently on changes, and has empathy for each other's objectives.

CYBERSECURITY EI (EMOTIONAL INTELLIGENCE) ENGINEER

What if cybersecurity positions were not solely focused on the implication of defensive measures, GRC, and risk management, but also with the emotional intelligence of security programs? As mentioned in previous sections, emotional intelligence could be integrated across the organization, but could be a specialty within a security engineering position. A Cybersecurity Emotional Intelligence Engineer (CEIE) could integrate empathy and emotional intelligence objectives between security teams and within policies. This individual may have a background in counseling or psychology, but with an interest in cybersecurity and technical pursuits. The CEIE could sit on a blue team or a red team, or between both teams in a purple team or working group. This individual would be responsible for integrating emotional intelligence principles into the security team, policies, and overall organization.

For example, a CEIE could work within the SOC as a consultant and advisor to analysts and network engineers on the team. A situation has arisen where users' machines have been contained with little information shared, leaving the users and their management teams frustrated. The SOC is equally as frustrated since they were containing a potentially more severe incident, and their security management team is aware of the type of attacks conducted. The SOC did not notify users until 3 minutes before containing their machines, leaving little time to save work or understand what is happening. The CEIE reviews the email messages, documents IR communication, and interacts with the users involved. Through this analysis, they teach the SOC analysts how to communicate with users more effectively, improve the IR communication chains to improve future incident response activities, as well as create email templates for different types of situations.

The CEIE could also work on a red team as part of the penetration test engagements. Red teams are typically focused on the social engineering, technical exploits available, and possible points of entry into systems. While the type of penetration test conducted will depend on the organization and the approved networks and systems, they may not include possible interactions with users or with the organization during and after the tests. Infrastructure and network engineers may feel frustrated or annoyed that the penetration test is taking place during several projects and maintenance activities. The CEIE would be aware of this and meet with the IT teams after the event to debrief them and request feedback to improve future engagements. This position allows for red teams to consider not just how to exploit users and systems, but how to collaborate with the technical and management staff of the organization.

CONCLUSION

Job titles and descriptions have been static for many years, and systems administrators and engineers, cybersecurity analysts, and network engineers have not changed a tremendous amount in this time. These positions have mostly changed in the required languages, types of technology used, or associated frameworks and guidelines to follow. This antiquated way of thinking leaves major gaps in the types of roles or skillsets that are needed in organizations today. Considering multidimensional roles that meet a variety of functions and can be across multiple teams only enhances the business. This also provides new and interesting career paths for technical and non-technical personnel within the organization.

With roles that combine human factors, psychological, security, operations, and development skillsets, organizations will mature faster than with traditional job roles. And one of the major benefits of roles like this is that an organization could take on one new job role for a liaison without a heavy lift. This individual would take one employee slot, and potentially serve several functions within their job description. It allows for career growth, unique opportunities, and encouraging personnel to stay within the organization and have mobility in different teams. What is the downside? Maybe it does not work immediately and takes some time to create change within the organization? This is a known quantity – but if organizations do not bring creativity into job roles, IT and cybersecurity personnel will continue to look for better opportunities.

Chapter 13

Building trust and new relationships

LETTING GO OF THE PAST

Let it go. Seriously, let it go. Executives, management, and technical professionals hold on to previous interactions, past policies, and perceptions based on communications. Perception-based decision-making is holding back organizations from maturing their IT and cybersecurity programs. Perception is how individuals understand situations based on their sensory inputs and may affect how they remember interactions. For example, if an IT operations group had a bad interaction with one individual in the Security Operations Center (SOC), their perception may be that any email from that team is negative. Without any context, if the perception is negative, the IT operations team may not want to respond to the security team or work with them on issues. A negative perception can be the single biggest concern with resolving security concerns and remediating vulnerabilities.

Simply with the awareness of how perception affects making decisions, perhaps with the aid of a Human Factors Security Engineer (HFSE), Human Factors IT Specialist (HFIS), or Cybersecurity Emotional Intelligence Engineer (CEIE), IT and security teams may reconsider how they interact with each other. If the IT manager encouraged their team to reconsider their interactions with security assessors/auditors, security assessments may run more efficiently with more risks being mitigated. For example, a development team has only had poor interactions in the past with the security team. The manager comes to the group and says that the security team and developers are going to start meeting every week until they can remediate outstanding risks. The manager hires a CEIE to run these meetings and help resolve past issues and encourage positive interactions while compromising on solutions.

Removing old perceptions and negative mindsets has more far-reaching implications than teamwork or collaboration. One positive interaction can lead to decreased time to identify and remediate vulnerabilities. Another interaction could lower the length of a security assessment from months to weeks. One meeting where the teams can come together and discuss projects may help identify potential conflicts or problems early on, leading to increased success in implementations. The possibilities are endless when negative perceptions turn into positive interactions, with individuals simply willing to interact with each other. There is not enough interest or pursuit of resolving problems with psychological or behavioral analysis techniques.

The industry talks about technical debt as the accumulation of old and antiquated hardware and software that is cumbersome on the organization. Old systems mean mountains of missing patches, End of Life (EOL) concerns, lack of functionality, and missed opportunities for improvements. The same is here of old perceptions of how the teams operate and function together. Consider this to be perception debt from interactions between IT and cybersecurity teams. Is there a technical gap? Absolutely. But the technical gap is also based in the communication, or lack of communication, between both teams. Letting go of old habits, interactions, and memories will open possibilities to improve both functionality and security objectives.

GETTING RID OF PRECONCEIVED NOTIONS

Take the idea of old perceptions a step further and apply it to the skills and technical requirements for job descriptions and positions. There are a lot of preconceived notions on the types of technical skills that make a candidate successful in IT and cybersecurity. This same notion applies to the required education levels or certifications required for IT or cybersecurity professionals. But if organizations continue to see the same types of cyberattacks being successful time and time again, there is a gap between what skills are believed to be essential, and what might be essential in this point in time.

The idea that someone with 20 certifications is far more qualified versus someone with one certification is a limiter on the available candidate pool. Someone with one certification could pass the same technical skills challenges and may have only had the opportunity to take one exam or was not as interested in certifications. Items like certifications or education are one element to an individual's profile, and to test the technical skill in an interview can be appropriate based on the type of role but should not be a sole factor in a candidates' success in a role. Technical IT and cybersecurity professionals cannot know every possible language or technology, but the ability to learn quickly and adapt can be even better skills. Even better, the ability to empathize and work well with other teams could help resolve long-standing tensions between teams, and ultimately move the technical needle further.

Similarly, the idea that someone with 20 years of experience versus someone with 1 year of experience would be better qualified is not always correct. It is possible an engineer with 20 years of experience would prefer to manage and implement technology the way they always have, instead of adapting skillsets and accommodating of constantly changing environments. A new graduate with a bachelor's degree in computer science with internship experience might not have the depth of technical skill but would be eager to learn and grateful for an opportunity to prove their technical abilities. These are two cases of what certifications and skills may look like for IT and cybersecurity positions, but the main point is that every individual has a different skillset. Preconceived notions about what someone can or cannot do solely based on one element within their resume could leave IT and cybersecurity programs at a standstill.

Another potentially dangerous preconceived notion is that cybersecurity teams are solely in place to say 'no' or to stop projects. This is simply not true. There are certainly some individuals and teams that operate that way, but that is an antiquated way of running a cybersecurity program. Cybersecurity teams are starting to adapt to enable the business, so if IT and development teams consider cybersecurity as a blocker, this could be damaging to the overall security of the organization. Instead, each team needs to stop seeing each other as blockers, and potential allies to accomplish mutual goals. Removing old stigmas can allow room for better communication and compromising on objectives, instead of stopping projects and affecting functionality for users.

The same goes with preconceived ideals about what technology is required to make an environment functional and consistently operational. The world of emerging technology changes so quickly and decisions may be made too quickly to change or remove tools and software in an environment, for example, removing a vulnerability scanning tool because of perceived missing functionality to replace it with a newer tool on the market. While the new tool may look like it has additional functionality or visibility into vulnerabilities, the current scanning tool may not be configured properly to provide maximum results. If the team could do a technical deep dive on the current scanning tool, they may find other ways of configuring settings and policies to provide the additional functionality.

APPROACHING PROJECTS IN A NEW WAY

There are many certification programs and educational opportunities available for IT and project management, including the Information Technology Infrastructure Library (ITIL) and Project Management Professional (PMP) certifications. These are great options to provide foundational knowledge on how to run projects for IT and cybersecurity teams. But these ideals should not be the 'end all, be all' to how to manage projects within an organization. Using project management techniques to organize tasks, assign resources, and determine timelines are important to help coordinate efforts across the organization. However, these should only be the starting point of how to organize projects. Also consider the coordination between teams, skillsets of team members, and others who may be able to assist, as well as potential impact on other systems.

For example, an IT project that is underway to remove and replace old network devices, re-work the network architecture, as well as improve the security of the environment by using micro-segmentation techniques. The project team would include the network engineering team, any architects, and some of the affected application and systems owners. These systems owners can help provide guidance and expertise on their own systems, as well as what network requirements they may have. The inclusion of these systems owners early on can help guide the architecture decisions. Security teams should also be included during the planning phase of this project, to help implement secure architecture design principles before any technical implementation. The inclusion of teams from the planning phase ensures both functionality and security goals are met early on, which will ultimately lead to a successful project.

Projects should also not be completely static, consider DevOps and chaos engineering principles when planning projects. DevOps groups combine development and operations teams during projects for the same reason IT and cybersecurity professionals need to collaborate. Before DevOps and agile methodologies, developers would create applications and send to operations teams for management. This left operations teams with little information on how the systems were created and difficult in managing them once deployed to production. These same challenges are why IT and cybersecurity teams do not always work well together or have contentious relationships. Using a DevOps approach to IT and security programs, or SecOps, could change the way cybersecurity teams interact and engage within IT projects.

Another approach to help change the way IT and cybersecurity teams interact is to integrate chaos engineering principles into projects. Chaos engineering is the use of a hypothesis-based methodology to test systems with the aim of building resiliency into those systems. For example, a chaos engineer may suspect that changing one setting on a network device may remove HA functionality between two switches. They would test that hypothesis, once approved, and monitor what happens with the systems. This helps to detect and prevent functionality concerns before something breaks in production and affects users unnecessarily. The chaos engineering methodology could be applied to security programs, as chaos security engineering. Similar to penetration tests, the idea would be to test security controls before a malicious actor would have an opportunity to exploit them. This changes the way IT and cybersecurity programs collaborate, and shifts security further left without fearing it in production environments.

EARLY AND OFTEN OPEN COMMUNICATION

IT and cybersecurity teams have experienced frustration and tension based on the lack of communication, which ultimately leads to late information which stalls projects. Integrating security teams late into a project means remediation of findings is left to right before a system goes into production. This could lead to failed projects, insecure configures placed into production, or systems that require longer term assessments which increase costs and may decrease revenue. Whether an impact to business or security, improving communication channels between teams will lead so successful and secure product deployments.

For example, a cybersecurity manager could introduce themselves to both the IT operations team lead and the development leads for both major applications managed by the organization. With this introduction, they provide background on what the team monitors and looks for within the environment. This demonstrates an openness to collaborate and would provide an introduction before an incident occurs. Introductions between the teams during a major cyber incident would be stressful. Instead, when an incident occurs, all the operations team know the manager and when they see something suspicious, they can notify the cybersecurity team quickly. A brief introduction like this one could lead to a long-term partnership and provide faster communications in the event of an incident.

Another example would be the cybersecurity engineering team making an introduction during an operations call with IT administrators. This call was set up by management to introduce the technical staff on both sides and encourage them to collaborate on projects. This initial engagement could encourage cybersecurity professionals to reach out to the IT team with questions on vulnerabilities, before sending a full report. The IT team would respond more positively to the incremental vulnerability information versus a listing of hundreds of vulnerabilities. The IT team may also feel more comfortable reaching out to the cybersecurity engineers when trying to remediate complex findings. Another partnership with information sharing that could remediate findings more quickly, and each team could provide their expertise to each other for other projects.

Communication does not have to occur during high stress situations like the end of a project or during a cybersecurity incident. Whether it takes place inside or outside of work, IT and cybersecurity teams have more in common than they may realize during daily activities. Both groups are highly technical, motivated, and fast learners with each field constantly evolving to support emerging tech. Instead of only focusing on project tasks and security assessments, these teams can help each other solve problems and resolve outstanding issues. IT operations groups may even rely on cybersecurity engineers or architects to help provide solutions once they compare skillsets. Cybersecurity professionals are technical and often come from IT backgrounds, and they would complement IT groups nicely and provide more than just security recommendations.

HAVE FUN WITH IT

As mentioned in the previous section, communications do not only need to occur between the groups during stressful times, like finalizing projects or when reacting to data breaches. Consider an organization where there are multiple critical vulnerabilities, EOL software the IT team is slowly working to upgrade, and several ongoing IT projects. This is stressful for any administrator; working with security teams to try and remediate critical vulnerabilities while upgrading systems and managing current systems for users. SOC teams are equally as stressed monitoring multiple tools, reviewing alerts, and responding to threats and malicious actors regularly to protect the organization. It is no secret that both IT and cybersecurity can be incredibly stressful roles. So why not add some fun?

Part of the increased tension between these groups is the high stress situations when they interact. So instead of solely focusing on these interactions, why not encourage brainstorming and 'think tank' meetings between projects. Innovation meetings help to break up some of the stress from daily tasking and help the teams discuss ongoing problems or concerns within the environment. Even if these items cannot be acted upon initially, there is room to allow the teams to engage on problem-solving and use their complementary technical skills in a different way. Not only is this a fun activity, but it encourages unity between the groups, and allows for career growth. There may also be new and interesting projects that come out of these brainstorming sessions that management bad not previously considered.

And to add a little fun and networking, why not have the IT and cybersecurity teams meet for lunches or after-work social hours? It is quite common for internal teams to socialize with their own groups outside of business hours, but why not bring these two teams together with social outings. IT or cybersecurity groups may go to conferences together with their individual teams, why not send one systems administrator and one security analyst instead? With their different educational and technical backgrounds, they may bring back unique perspectives from the conference. And while gathering information from sessions, they might also have fun and create a more casual relationship to bring back to the office.

There are no down sides to encouraging these teams to socialize and network with each other. They may learn new skills, improve their empathy and understanding for other groups, and have a better understanding of the overall business strategy. And with the 'Great Resignation', huge gaps in cybersecurity jobs waiting to be filled, couldn't integrating a little fun into stressful positions be beneficial to the employee's mental health as well? Improved mental health and better relationships affect so many components within the organization in a positive way. This takes typical business practices and challenges the way tradition IT and cybersecurity teams interact with one another.

CONSIDERING THE OTHER SIDE

At the core of change between IT and cybersecurity groups is the ability to empathize and understand each other's positions. Several the problems between these teams are the inability to understand tasking, projects, and mission. A compounding factor are the differences in education and technical experience that led to mistrust or disagreements. Empathy and emotional intelligence can help to bridge that gap, but there needs to be a business strategy in place that helps to align these teams. Executive management and leadership need to be involved with technical practitioners, since they develop and steer policies and procedures.

What if security awareness training for administrators introduced the members of the security team, their skillsets, and role on the team. The training could provide their contact information and technical expertise for questions on remediation. For example, a security engineer could be introduced with a specialization in java and python security experience. Or a security analyst could be presented showing their focus in vulnerability management and remediation capabilities. This introduction humanizes the security team and provides contact information to the IT operations team. It also changes the format for security training that the IT team may have seen year after year.

What if the security team received an introductory training to the various IT groups and development teams they would support within the organization? Typical employees would receive HR training, personnel record management, medical and other benefits, but not information on the teams they would collaborate with. For specific teams, why not introduce them to the organizational structure and typical systems they would provide security consultation and monitoring for? Introductory training for employees is very standardized, and customization could be included that help to provide context for the teams they would interact with. Then IT and cybersecurity teams are introduced to their counterparts early on in their employment, instead of at critical or stressful times.

IT teams could also provide introductions during onboarding for cybersecurity personnel. Consider an SOC analyst who is just joining the team, and this is their first experience managing and monitoring alerts. The environment is new, and they are unsure of what systems they are monitoring, other than seeing a stream of IPs and hostnames. If there was an initial technical architecture and network diagram presented to the new SOC analyst, along with system owner and technical Point of Contact (POC) information, this would help them to identify appropriate technical POCs. This introduction makes it an easier adjustment for SOC analysts who may not know the IT engineers and administrators behind the systems that they are monitoring. All of these types of interactions and methods for communication humanize the analysts, engineers, and developers behind the technical documentation and training.

IMPROVE SECURITY AND FUNCTIONALITY

There is this idea in the industry that security is a blocker, or IT operations group will not remediate vulnerabilities because of user requirements. This negativity permeates the idea that you can only meet user or security requirements, instead of being able to achieve both sets of goals. Instead of

Figure 13.1 Improving security and functionality.

focusing on negative or possibly complicated solutions, why not consider how security and functionality can meet in the middle. There are many configurations within systems that can meet both objectives, which alleviates issues for both teams. Instead of arguing over which controls to implement, maybe consider which ones can resolve multiple concerns. This is another area where the teams can come together and create a remediation plan that works for both IT and cybersecurity (Figure 13.1).

For example, an IT team has been struggling with multiple critical vulnerabilities on EOL systems. They have not upgraded because of the downtime required to upgrade both the OS and application-level vulnerabilities. But when they meet with the security team, both groups come up with a plan to create new servers on the latest versions of both the OS and the application. This allows the old environment to stay active to support users, while creating a new secure-by-design environment that will also enhance the functionality for users. With the later versions of the user-facing application, they can increase productivity and decrease workloads. A project like this removes the stigma of 'fix it now', and instead allows both teams to work together to find a viable solution.

Another example would be the adoption of cloud within an organization. They are moving their final on-premises and physical systems to a cloud infrastructure which supports several automation and security requirements. Both the IT and cybersecurity team can collaborate on the security architecture design behind the cloud environment. This solves a variety of problems, including easier deployment and management of servers (which decreases administrative overhead), enhanced security functionality (with the consultation from the security team), and less time to troubleshoot issues for users (which improves user productivity levels). Security does not have to be an 'either/or' decision in IT projects, and with proper communication and collaboration, both teams can have it all.

CHANGING MEETING STRUCTURE

Users need to have mobility and access to their business documents and applications on laptops, tablets, cell phones, and other mobile devices. After dealing with increased telework due to the pandemic, typical workdays in the office are forever changed. General and administrative users need to work from home, on the road, while traveling, and anywhere they may be supporting customers or clients. With these changes in the everyday work life, IT and cybersecurity professionals need flexible hours to manage and monitor systems and support users outside of classical 'business hours'. Typical meetings and the way they are organized do not fully support the needs of both teams. Instead, consider a few other options to help support how technical teams operate and function in today's customer-support model.

Even outside of IT and cybersecurity teams, meetings can be long and not as useful for technical staff. While it is important for teams to work together and discuss tasking and projects, why not consider a new way of meeting? Instead of an hour-long meeting every day to go over the days tasks, why not use team collaboration tools where the IT and cybersecurity teams can discuss. For example, consider an application for team messaging that includes channels and areas for group discussions. Why not have a channel or location for 'IT/Cyber Updates' or 'IT/Cyber Collaboration' so that the teams can ask each other questions, provide updates or changes on projects, as well as new technology integration into the environment.

Instead of meeting to go over these updates, they could be provided within the channel and then have a meeting to discuss any questions or comments on the updates. This saves time for providing the updates and focuses more on areas that need further discussion or collaboration. For example, consider a security assessment for a new system that the systems engineers and security assessors/auditors need to finish by the end of the next month. They use a channel to discuss any outstanding findings, provide remediation evidence, ask questions, and can collaborate much faster without daily or weekly meetings. Of course, meetings may still be required to keep tasking on track or discuss complex issues, but for the easier task items it makes more sense to use a collaboration platform instead.

Using channels or business communication applications allows for faster communications, instead of waiting for individuals to respond to emails. An IT/cybersecurity collaboration channel could also be used outside of security assessments, and for general interactions. When an IT team is given a new set of security standards they must meet, they could easily reach out to the cybersecurity team and ask questions. They could use this to verify settings, work on timelines for remediation, and coordinate vulnerability scans or reports. Meetings could then be structured around any challenges the team is facing, instead of focusing on tasking. Innovation and creative endeavors are better suited for live communication, so instead of focusing on day-to-day items, the meetings can be structured around problem-solving.

REMOVE SILOED GROUPS

Even within cybersecurity programs, teams may not always communicate with each other often enough to know what projects are ongoing, what vulnerabilities or risks there are in the environment, or holistically what the cyber hygiene of the network is. For example, consider a team of about 40 cybersecurity professionals who span security assessors/auditors, SEs, threat intelligence analysts, SOC analysts, and security architects. While the overall goal of each team is to enhance security through prevention, detection, and response, each team would have their objectives. Security assessors/auditors are focused on documentation and security assessments, while the SOC is concerned with active alerts and monitoring the network. An SOC analyst would not necessarily know how a security assessment went for a production system, as security assessors/auditors would not be expected to know what the day-to-day malicious alerts look like.

If it is difficult for members within the security teams to understand and appreciate other's ongoing tasks, it is increasingly more difficult for anyone outside of the team to do the same. So instead of having siloed teams who do not interact together, consider how teams could work together in a variety of ways. Have the entire cybersecurity program come together regularly to discuss ongoing projects, any outstanding risks, and any other concerns with projects that teams could work together on. If teams are able to meet each other regularly, and even in a networking or social context, this provides more open channels to communicate when there are questions or concerns in a project.

For example, consider the SOC and assessor team example, where the SOC does not know what security assessments are ongoing and what that means for the network. If a system had major vulnerabilities, EOL, or misconfigured settings, notifying the SOC would help them tailor alerts for those systems. Maybe they would increase logging for specific event IDs to identify IOCs, or maybe monitor that system more heavily than other systems until the critical vulnerabilities can be resolved. Without knowing that the risk is much higher on that particular system, how would the SOC know to be concerned about specific types of exploits? Maybe there is an EOL version of SQL installed that leaves a risk for SQL injection. If the SOC is notified or aware of this concern, they can tailor their alert configuration to enhance SQL injection detection. This is one example of how communication between the teams can help increase the security posture of the network.

Another example would be in the event of a major cybersecurity breach within the organization. Without knowing who the system owners are, or who to contact, precious time is spent with managers and cybersecurity professionals to reach the right individuals. If the system owners had regular meetings with the SOC managers and cybersecurity team leads, the channel of communication is open both directions. SOC members can notify system owners of potentially suspicious activity, and the system owners can reach out to the SOC when they detect something strange. These relationships are incredibly important to mature cybersecurity programs, and they are not considered vulnerabilities or security configurations in a technical sense. We need to consider how vulnerability and risk management are more than the technology we deploy, but the human connections that utilize that technology.

ENCOURAGE COLLABORATION

This section on encouraging collaboration between teams cannot be highlighted enough. This has been a running theme throughout because of the significance it plays on the success or failure of a cybersecurity program. Encouraging collaboration must be a top-down strategy that is shown from executive management down to middle and lower tiers of management. If the executive level and management do not encourage collaboration through their own partnerships, how can they expect the other teams to follow suit. If the CIO and CISO are constantly at odds in their views and vision, neither group will be able to succeed fully or experience a mature program. But if the CIO and CISO can bring their teams together for regular meetings, share their experiences, and encourage teamwork between operations and security, they will positively impact both of their groups.

For example, IT teams are under pressure to deliver consistent and functional systems to their users or customers. To do this, they must constantly resolve issues, integrate properly with other systems, and work on enhancing the infrastructure to improve usability. All these goals must be met while also trying to meet the appropriate security standard for the organization. If the CIO feels that security is a burden and limiting the IT team, this perspective will trickle down to the systems administrators and engineers that manage the systems. They will be told that security is a secondary function and to focus on their users first. However, if the CIO saw that an early collaboration with security teams led to successful IT projects, they would change the way the organization felt about security. The CIO could hold conjoint meetings for both the CIO and CISO office, showing both teams that their goals are aligned.

There is a misconception that working in combination means that they must agree on every subject. This is simply not true – disagreement can be done in a professional manner that allows growth for both teams. The security team may not believe that users should have access to certain websites, and that the organization should adopt an 'accepted list' of websites versus an 'unaccepted list'. This would severely restrict the number of websites that users could access, and may affect their functionality, especially when traveling to customer sites or requirements for research. While the two teams disagree, they come to a compromise where the 'unaccepted list' is more comprehensive and dynamic, allowing for faster updates when malicious websites are identified. This meets the constantly changing security requirements for websites that are constantly changing, while also reducing the chances of blocking a relevant website for users.

Encouraging collaboration between IT and cybersecurity teams does not need to be a heavy lift for management, starting with one meeting between the CIO, CISO, and their upper-level management. For smaller organizations, if there is no CISO, having the CIO discuss the important of security with IT operations and engineering groups. It is the start of changing the way teams think and operate with each other. This also means that the CISO would need to encourage a positive relationship with IT, providing consultation and expertise, instead of blocking projects. The older way of viewing cybersecurity as a blocker for projects changes when security teams embrace the functionality and user requirements of the business. There needs to be a positive push-pull between the groups, which starts with management encouragement and the ability to try something new.

BUILDING TRUST

Trust is not built overnight. Collaboration will not occur after one or even five meetings. Building positive relationships between IT and cybersecurity will take time and effort to change the way people feel about the other teams. It will take regular meetings, changing meeting formats, encouraging new project management techniques, and a host of other tools to affect how teams collaborate. Building trust in any relationship takes time and can be done in a variety of ways between the teams. Whether it is providing expertise outside of normal projects, coming up with creative solutions, or socializing outside of work hours, each of these elements can bring teams together and encourage problem-solving instead of simply rejecting each other's requests.

For example, providing expertise outside of projects or ongoing tasks can be an excellent relationship builder and increase trust. If IT teams do not trust the cybersecurity teams technical abilities, there is an opportunity to prove this expertise while increasing trust. Take a scenario where the IT team is working on integrating a new mail system while decommissioning the old one. The IT team wants to improve the security of the system based on recommended guidance, but one of the settings is breaking authentication for users. The security team, while not directly involved on this project, is notified by their management that the email team is having trouble applying the specified security controls. The security engineers arrange a meeting and determine the required setting will not work properly for this system, and they recommend mitigating controls that will resolve the finding. This situation helps the project progress, resolves an outstanding security finding, and demonstrates the flexibility and willingness to collaborate from the security team.

Another option for building trust between the teams is for security teams to come up with creative solutions for the IT team. Security standards can be somewhat rigid and identify only one option for remediation, which leaves IT groups stuck to either resolve or request an exemption or waiver for that finding. This type of remediation limits what IT groups can do, and may result in more waivers and unresolved vulnerabilities, versus the findings being addressed as dictated by the security standards. If security teams, such as security assessors/auditors and SEs, can provide alternative mitigations to the security findings, this allows IT teams flexibility to align functionality and security goals. Allowing for creativity also shows the ability for the security team to adapt and collaborate with the IT team, instead of only offering one option to meet security controls.

A final option for IT and cybersecurity teams to build trust is to encourage networking and outside work socializing. If teams only interact during business hours, and as mentioned previously, during stressful situations, it would be incredibly difficult to build trust. Consider a monthly outing for both the IT and cybersecurity teams to meet either for a brainstorming lunch or after hours at an event. And not just a 'happy hour' where everyone meets at a bar – get creative. Why not invite everyone to a local concert or to a sporting event? Or consider hosting a chess tournament between the groups if all members are online and in different locations. Look to your teams to identify what hobbies or interests may align between both teams. There are multiple opportunities to build trust outside of a traditional lunch or happy hour.

Chapter 14

Path forward

THE PROBLEM

IT and cybersecurity groups are at odds based on their perceived differences in technical skills, goals, and objectives within the organization. Education in IT programs is focused on mastering the tools, technology, and methodologies required for operations and engineering programs. In stark contrast, security educational pursuits are focused on security frameworks, technologies, and associated risk management activities. IT and cybersecurity individuals who start a career after pursuing higher level education or certification training opportunities learn only their field. While this is completely necessary to build a foundation of knowledge, cybersecurity is an elective or concentration that is available for IT or computer science degrees. Cybersecurity programs do not currently teach or focus on the operational environments and business strategy.

Businesses and IT teams see security as a challenge or a blocker to finishing projects on time and achieving a functional environment. Security teams are considerably understaffed and underbudgeted, leaving a lack of personnel able to handle secure configuration, assessment, continuous monitoring, and incident response activities. IT teams must adhere to security frameworks or face penalties during audits or failed projects due to critical outstanding vulnerabilities. While security teams are trying to identify vulnerabilities, adhere to multiple security frameworks, and evolve to an ever-changing landscape of exploits and threats. Both teams are stressed, frustrated, and are not always poised for successful interactions on projects, given their conflicting goals.

These conflicting goals are seen during projects, tasking, and meetings when each team is fighting for their own objectives. IT teams must support their users and customer base, by ensuring uptime and meeting Service Level Agreement (SLA) requirements. While security teams are focused on enhancing security and reducing risk of the organization, while adhering to security frameworks like the Center for Internet Security (CIS) benchmarks or SOC (System and Organization Controls) report at level 1, 2, or 3. If IT groups are unable to meet security requirements based on EOL hardware or software that is supporting users, the security team may grow frustrated. Likewise, the

IT team may feel constrained by the amount of security controls and remediations they must constantly investigate and implement.

These two teams have not been given a framework for functioning well together by design. While it is possible that these two teams already work well, in traditional implementations this design is not indicative of a collaborative space for teams. Even with the tools they manage, IT and cybersecurity software may be at odds and impact functionality for users. For example, an antivirus or anti-malware tool may impact virtual services or servers. And from the security side they may be limited with what they can accomplish without executive management and leadership support from the organization. All these issues compound the problems and concerns between IT and cybersecurity teams. As mentioned, this does not mean that IT, development, and cybersecurity teams cannot collaborate, but it will take time to improve relationships and align goals.

It is important to note that not every organization experiences this issue, it may be small scale or on a larger scale that impedes both groups. However, it is crucial for leadership and practitioners to examine their relationships with other teams and see if these issues exist. It is possible that this is not just the operations and security team, but between the development and security team. Maybe the security team is having trouble working with data scientists and researchers because of ongoing project requirements or timelines. The main problem is the differing objectives and limitations that security teams may be experiencing between other groups, but specifically operations-focused teams.

BRIDGING THE TECHNICAL GAP

Technical skills, tools, and applications available for each team can also lead to the challenges between teams. IT groups use technology to support users, enhance their administrative capabilities, and automate manual processes. Security teams use technology to monitor systems, identify malicious or suspicious behavior, and detect misconfigurations and missing controls. IT teams are trained in implementing, upgrading, migrating, and managing the daily operations of their tools and systems. Security groups are trained to look for anomalous behavior with alerts and network activity, review vulnerabilities and controls, and deploy secure development practices. For example, an IT administrator would be concerned with the migration of new email services to enhance use functionality, whereas the security team would be interested in the decommissioning of End of Life (EOL) systems and mitigating numerous vulnerabilities.

The technology focus of each team is quite different, but they can learn so much from each other if given the opportunity to work together. No one person can know everything about technical implementation and security, given the fast pace that each field is changing. Given the increased complexity behind hybrid systems, integration of Artificial Intelligence/Machine Learning (AI/ML) technologies, and development environments, IT and security teams are constantly under pressure to learn. Through the encouragement of collaboration and open channels of communication, IT and cybersecurity teams can share the technical knowledge they have with each other. This allows for resolution of the increasingly complex problems with the webs of technology weaved through an organization. But bridging the technical gap is not quite as focused on the tools, applications, and systems within an environment, but more so on the practitioners that use them.

Understanding increasingly complex environments is an ability that all technical and cybersecurity practitioners must adopt. This complexity runs vertically through the organization in the number of applications that work in combination, as well as horizontally as infrastructure and systems are stacked and depend on each other. To add security frameworks and regulations, new types of threats and exploits adds even more layers to the technology onion. But technology and security do not have to have competing goals which create conflict and tension between teams. When security and risk management are aligned with technical projects and strategic goals, functionality and operations groups can work harmoniously to integrate their tools and applications. From management down to the practitioners, it is important to keep an open mind on the depth of technical skill and abilities between teams.

Without appreciation for each other's technical skills, and even gaps, teams will continue to be misaligned and lack behind other organizations. And similarly, without an understanding of moving targets related to security incidents, IT and security teams will have difficult adapting to and reacting to malicious events. For example, consider the SolarWinds and Log4j incidents, information about those zero-day events was changing daily and even hourly, over many months. Security teams worked closely with operations and development teams to give the most up to date and accurate remediation information. Although these were tense situations, if both groups worked in tandem, they would be able to resolve the concerns quickly and efficiently.

HUMAN FIRST

As discussed, *technology* and *process* are often discussed first and at the forefront of resolving problems within organizations. And while these are both incredibly important to align, organizations often forget the most important element behind the functionality and security of their technology, *people*. Tools, applications, and devices are built by humans, with the intention of humans to use them. Applicability of technology to people may not seem like an important note for organizations and is deemed a common understanding.

This could be considered a throwaway or well-known concept without giving much thought to how it applies to the implementation of the technology and processes. But this is an incredible mistake if the technology cannot be utilized properly, or the processes do not make sense for the people of the organization.

People are as complex as the technology and processes that are used throughout an enterprise. Users are driven by their business and job requirements, personal and professional goals, as well as educational or knowledge pursuits. But this is just the surface-level of what makes up a user, they also are driven by the needs of their team and ongoing projects and tasking. For example, an IT administrator is focused on the maintenance of their systems based on SLAs, but also by the drive to learn more about a new technology or methodology, like quantum computing. A security analyst is driven by the accuracy and high load of events and analysis that must be done quickly to detect events, while maybe also considering what it would be like to learn to be a security engineer. People are multi-faceted, and the technology and processes that they must use and adhere to can either enable them, or negatively impact their productivity.

Users are also ruled by the perceptions, biases, and experiences they have had throughout their careers. Considering people, technology, or processes as one moment in time limits the understanding of complexity of each piece of this puzzle. Biases and perceptions do not need to have a negative impact on IT and cybersecurity programs, but with awareness and insight, can in fact improve them. Understanding that a system owner may have had a prior negative experience with security allows the security team to develop a plan to improve that relationship. Without this willingness to adapt to that situation and change their strategy, they will continue to see the same patterns of frustration and stagnated security practices. On the IT side, more understanding on how security teams operate and that they do not want to be blockers on projects can also improve and strengthen relationships.

Understanding how psychology plays into the habits, behavior, and interactions between employees would improve both IT and cybersecurity programs. The consultation from behavioral analysis or cognitive psychologists would provide advice on the current state of the organization, as well as what changes could be made to improve internal practices. Many other fields, like competitive athletic sports, use behavioral analysis techniques to change unhealthy habits to improve performance. For example, consider a security analyst who has a habit of switching quickly between applications without really digesting the alerts and information they see. Having a psychological consultation to interact with analysts, they determine that there are far too many tools to monitor and leave the analyst missing alerts. This helps the security group determine the root cause of missing alerts, not that they are poor performers, but that they simply have too much on their plate to be able to act on.

BEHAVIORAL ANALYSIS TECHNIQUES

Behavioral analysis is specifically the study of understanding how humans behave to help break bad habits and build healthy and positive habits (Siu et al., 2019). There are multiple techniques that behavioral analysts and psychologists use to identify and change behaviors in people. For example, to improve the performance of competitive athletes, the analysts may determine that the only thing holding back athletic performance is the regularity of practice between mandated practices with the team. The analysts may suggest a slow increase to adding 10 minutes of additional practice, to 12 minutes, to then 15 minutes additional a day to change how the athlete spends time on practice. This incremental form of behavioral change encourages change slowly and at a pace that leads to longevity in positive habits.

For example, in a technology context, consider a developer who learned some bad coding habits during their first job out of college. Maybe it was just a coworker who taught them some shortcuts or encouraged insecure practices to get projects done. Or maybe it was a project manager who pushed for developers to get their work done on time, regardless of quality. Either way, the developer walks into their next job and this new organization has hired a behavioral analysis psychologist to evaluate how the development teams interact and follow best practices. Through determining that this new developer had gained some bad habits from a past position, they work to provide best practices and monitor the developers code at the end of every week to see if they are changing their habits. Through some encouragement and instruction on better coding practices, the developer gains some new skills as well as increase the quality of their work products. Win – win – win.

In a security program, consider a threat intelligence analyst who is new to their full-time position after graduating with a bachelor's degree in information assurance. In their undergraduate program they learned several the methodologies behind looking for and utilizing open-source threat intelligence information. But they did not necessarily have the hands-on usage of the technical tools used at the organization, which meant they did not have the practice with using automation to their advantage. While this is not a bad habit, it can be an opportunity to inherit good habits by learning management and operations of those tools within that environment. If there is a solid documentation and up-front training to encourage positive behaviors when investigating and managing the tools available, it sets up the analyst for good work habits throughout their career. It is also entirely possible that based on the initial training and willingness to teach a young professional hire, that individual would be more willing to stay at the company long term.

Behavioral analysis techniques are not only applicable to IT and security practitioners, but also the users and integrating into the security program as well. Security training can be enhanced incredibly by the integration of changing habits and behavior of users, instead of using the common learning methodologies. These techniques can also be used to increase training for administrators and system owners, to help them learn how to use the technology available to them appropriately. For example, administrators or other users with privileged access should be receiving regular training as well and encouraging building positive habits can also improve security. These are just a few methods of delivery for behavioral analysis techniques into training, and they can also be integrated into meeting structure and organizational processes.

There are numerous behavioral analysis techniques available to help IT and cybersecurity personnel to develop new skills, understand their own behaviors, and ultimately improve the way they perform their duties. But these techniques can also be used to understand user behavior and employed by the security team to enhance any security awareness training or when interacting with users during an incident. IR teams and the communication chain during incidents are a great fit for using these techniques since the individuals must coordinate quickly and efficiently during an event. Determining potential concerns within these communication channels can improve the way teams work together in stressful situations, as well as the speed of identification to containment.

TECHNOLOGY AND SECURITY SECOND

When we consider the *people* behind all our teams, including security, IT, data scientists, development, HR, and administration, the organization aligns them with the *technology* and *processes* already in place. Consider the processes, guidance, and policies within the organization – are there far too many for personnel to be able to read and digest? Is there conflicting information that makes it difficult for users to understand the IT and security policies? Are users given proper instruction on how to use and manage their systems? Do system owners have the guidance available to understand the associated security considerations and requirements? This is a larger-scale concern with the IT and security guidance provided to users, but the point is, are the policies and processes written with the users in mind?

For IT groups, the consideration is for how the administrators, engineers, and architects are supported as the people who manage the infrastructure and systems. Administrators and engineers are not the SLAs, customer requirements, and skills that make up a person, but individuals with thoughts and ideas on the systems they manage. If these individuals are not encouraged to innovate, share ideas and thoughts, they can become frustrated with performing the same tasks each day. Each administrator and engineer have different skillsets, creative solutions, and abilities to improve the environment if they are encouraged to do this. If management and executive leadership can understand the personality types of interests of the IT team that works with them, they can encourage these innovative endeavors while managing their systems.

For security teams, the same is very much true for personality types and skillsets that each analyst, engineer, and architect may possess. One of the interesting things about the cybersecurity community are the passionate and inspired people that want to secure systems. There is a common thirst for knowledge, self-taught techniques, and willingness to learn new tools and technology at a rapid pace. Even given the many domains within cybersecurity, analysts and engineers are highly motivated to protect networks and solve complex problems. This is a commonality between IT and cybersecurity groups, and these appetites for knowledge could be a great avenue to bridge the technical gap between teams. These two teams do not have to be at odds for the mission that they support but could collaborate and share knowledge to mature both sets of goals.

Even in smaller organizations with one IT administrator and one security analyst. If they are constantly at odds over vulnerability findings and remediation efforts or disagreeing over what technical implementation is best, the organization will not be able to optimize either team. In medium-sized organizations, if the security team is considered an impediment to improving technology, the risks are incredibly higher for a security incident. And in a medium-sized business, if there is little security-focus or remediation of vulnerabilities, a security incident could be devastating to the business or reputation. But if the organization instead considered the people behind the IT and cybersecurity groups, they would effectively improve the technology and processes across the tech stack.

VERTICAL AND LATERAL CHANGES

Changing behavior, collaboration, communication, and teamwork between both IT and cybersecurity teams is not an overnight process. Nor can it be done by one team, or by executive management and leadership alone. Improving relationships between these groups requires changes both vertically and laterally throughout organizations. From the helpdesk to security analysts and engineers, to the data scientists that use the IT infrastructure, technical practitioners need to be part of that shifting mindset. There is a lot of current research and literature on the topic of executive management and leadership to improve cybersecurity programs. This is absolutely one important component to improve security, but mindsets and relationships between IT and cybersecurity groups also need to evolve.

IT groups, whether operations, engineering, or architecture, need to consider security teams as allies and remove old stigmas behind implementing security controls. In the past, security may have been a paperwork exercise or more cumbersome for IT groups, but it does not have to continue in that direction. Security can enable the business and the technology that the IT team utilizes and manages. But this mindset must be applied across IT teams, from the inclusion of security during the onset of projects, collaborating during remediation activities, and consulting when developing new products. IT management needs to encourage the early and often communication between the groups for this strategy to succeed. This is not a one-way collaborative effort, it must move up and down, and horizontally throughout the enterprise.

Security groups cannot focus solely on the risk management activities, vulnerability identification and remediation, and security alerts and response. While these are of most importance to the group, the security teams can consider how security impacts the functionality and operability of IT teams and systems. All vulnerabilities throughout the environment will never be remediated, it is simply not possible. But more vulnerabilities are remediated, and security controls implemented, when a positive relationship exists between IT and security groups. When security teams and management make themselves available for consultation and creative solutions for findings, it encourages IT teams to collaborate on more remediation efforts. Even one instance of a security team identifying mitigating controls instead of forcing remediation by patching, upgrading, or applying specific settings. Identified vulnerabilities may provide one or maybe two remediation options, however, there can be other mitigating controls to explore if both IT and security teams work together to resolve.

Even a positive relationship between IT and security management groups can trickle down to the practitioners on both sides. This initial relationship, or even willingness to communicate, has a positive chain effect down to the practitioners on their teams. An initially horizontal change between management can lead to a vertical effect down through the organization. And even considering how the IT and security teams interact with users and customers, do they have support and visibility? Even improving communications from the IT and security teams to the users help with awareness and support of their collective objectives.

CURRENT STATE

IT and security teams are at odds and have difficulty collaborating based on their differing goals, skillsets, and support through the organization. Both teams were not necessarily built to work together on projects by design, which has inhibited projects on either side. Whether it is lack of support from executive management and leadership, different views on high priority projects, or what is important for the organization to focus on, these teams are at odds. Practitioners receive very different types and levels of education, have

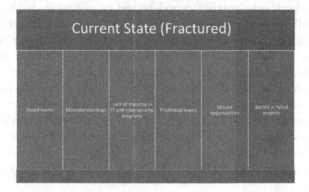

Figure 14.1 Insert diagram – current fractured state.

years of experience that affect their perspectives, and even opposing goals from each other. IT and cybersecurity groups do not necessarily walk in to either career with biases or perceptions, but after a few experiences in competing projects, these experiences will impact future interactions between teams (Figure 14.1).

Regardless of the size of teams, IT and cybersecurity groups are both incredibly overloaded by business objectives, user requirements, and constantly evolving technical implementations. All while learning new frameworks, guidelines, and increasingly complex infrastructures to manage and secure. This does not mean that security is not important to IT, or that operations concerns are not important to security teams. But it does mean that each group will work on their own objectives first and consider the other team as secondary. While this is a typical occurrence, it is one of the factors that leads to contention and frustration between the teams, ultimately resulting in complex relationships between IT and cybersecurity. However, these are not the only impacts to both groups.

Current cybersecurity teams are typically underfunded, understaffed, and not always supported by other teams and upper-level management. Even with the best intentions, vulnerabilities may be left unresolved to support antiquated applications and systems, because of IT functionality or user requirements. Risks are waived or exempted because of needs of the user, customer, or business. This puts organizations at risk for increased security incidents, failed audits or numerous audit findings, or inability to meet required frameworks. It may also lead to failed IT or development projects or putting insecure applications and systems into production. There are complex and compounding issues that come from the lack of collaboration between IT and cybersecurity teams.

Another note on the current state of IT and cybersecurity relationships is simply the lack of awareness of what each team does during the day.

This leaves both sides unable to understand or empathize with each other. Projects stall, disagreements arise over one or two findings, and either team may be lacking in awareness of projects and tasks. Without this awareness, teams are focused on their own objectives and planning installs and upgrades without sharing the information with each other. Security teams may be unaware of new systems until they are ready for production, instead of being involved from the decision to purchase that technology. IT teams may find out at the end of a project that they must meet specific security guidelines, without the understanding of requirements from the onset. These late interactions lead to fractured relationships and missed opportunities for improvements on both sides.

DESIRED STATE

While the words between IT and cybersecurity will never be a utopia, there are certainly many improvements that can be made to the programs, relationships, and projects between the two groups. Ideally, the two teams would be able to collaborate early and often on projects. Each team of practitioners would have the budget, resources, and tools required to build the best and more secure environments possible. They could politely disagree on security configurations and still lower their risk profile across the network. Executive management would fully support and encourage both groups to collaborate and provide the appropriate budgets to each team. However, this is an idyllic state, a much more realistic place for IT and cybersecurity will be open communication, empathy, and understanding, and will take some time for organizations to put into place.

As far as the *technology* goes between IT and cybersecurity groups, implementing security by design in products would go a long way to resolve a number of the issues mentioned in previous sections. If hardware, software, cloud platforms, and applications came with security built in, and allowed administrators to remove settings based on their environment, it would alleviate a lot of the manual process of adding security once a product is purchased. The same goes for development practices, DevSecOps is a relatively new concept, but it would be more prudent to consider SecDevOps as a standard within the community. A security first mindset, which can be cultivated during training and education programs, would alleviate several the last-minute security findings and remediation efforts.

For the *process* component of organizations, the documentation, guidance, and policies must encourage and enforce security requirements. Security policies must provide technical and easily implementable controls and configurations. Documents that give general guidance leave the implementation up to the administrators and would not provide any standardization for security controls throughout the network. Consider an organization with multiple cloud deployments managed by different groups. Without standardized security guidance on Identity and Access Management (IAM), Operating System (OS) and application baselines, and automation considerations, administrators would come up with their own solutions to these policies. While this is not necessarily a bad thing, it does make security assessments, remediation efforts, and overall security a moving target for these systems. Polices must be comprehensive, but succinct, and provide a maturity model for administrators to follow.

And finally, the *people* piece of the puzzle. This is a much more complex area that will require the most work. The technology can be configured, the policies can be updated, but the *people* in any organization will take time to adjust to new requirements. Users, administrators, developers, analysts, engineers, and architects all come from different backgrounds, education levels, and varying professional experience. The desired state would be centered around embracing the different backgrounds of the individuals in the organization. Using those differing skillsets to the advantage of pushing both IT and cybersecurity goals forward, instead of constantly combatting over projects and findings. But this takes time, organizations would need to focus on what the desired state is and create a roadmap for how to achieve that. This would vary quite a bit, given that each organization would have its own concerns and impediments (Figure 14.2).

Harmony is possible between the *people*, *processes*, and *technology* of an organization. The first step is awareness that there may be more concerns than the tools or security policy. Understanding how perception affects decision-making, how empathy positively impacts organizations, and how teams work better when they align all three components is the ultimate state of progress. This requires considerations and action up and down in the organization, but that change starts with executive management. Once the executive leadership shows a willingness to collaborate and change

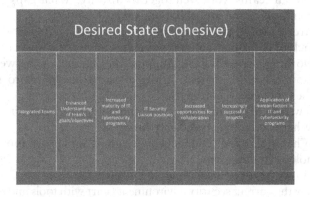

Figure 14.2 Desired state.

the way they operate, practitioners see this change and can start to adapt accordingly. Again, this is not an overnight change, but something that can be built over time. Trust and understanding take time to build in any relationship, and between IT and cybersecurity teams is no different.

HOW CAN WE GET THERE?

Positive change is possible for organizations to help bridge the technical gaps between IT and cybersecurity teams. While this roadmap and desired state will look different for each organization, here are a few steps to get groups started. Before any of these steps can take place, the IT and cybersecurity teams must first be willing to work together and identify that they may be biased or had bad experiences in the past. The idea is to understand that relationships can change, and those relationships can positively impact their working experience. It can also have a profound impact on the security and functionality of the environment, given that each team tries to change the way they work together. This willingness to identify potential issues and accept our own limitations is the most crucial step to being able to do this. And without executive management and leadership support, this project would never get off the ground.

The following list will provide a maturity model, of sorts, for what executive leadership can do to foster the relationships between IT and cybersecurity. Even if the conversation starts between the leadership of the IT and cybersecurity teams, or between the CIO and CISO, this is critical to the success of this undertaking. Each step will have a list of questions to begin conversations and help management start to determine the root of the problems.

1. IT and cybersecurity leadership initial meeting to discuss potential concerns
   a. Do our teams work well together already? What gaps are there in communication and collaboration?
   b. Are security teams impeding out current IT efforts? Why? Is it a lack of coordination between teams during the onset of projects?
   c. Do our current policies support the interaction between teams? Do we provide enough information to our teams to implement these policies accordingly?
2. Review the current infrastructure and ongoing IT projects
   a. What is ongoing? Is security involved?
   b. What is planned? Did security weigh in our chosen tools and technology in development?
   c. Do we have too many ongoing projects?
3. Review the current security environment (start with tools and technology)
   a. Do we have too many tools? Is this too difficult to manage?

   b. How mature are our practices and do we have the tools to do what
       we need to do?
4. Review IT teams (resources, budgets, and personnel)
   a. Do our teams have the required technical skills to manage AND
       secure our infrastructure? Can we upskill or provide more train-
       ing to help?
   b. Do our IT teams have the appropriate budget to properly imple-
       ment and manage their systems?
   c. Do they have an appreciation for security? Do they see it as an
       impediment?
5. Review security teams (resources, budgets, and personnel)
   a. Are we supporting our security teams to achieve their mission?
   b. Have we provided enough budget to the security teams to manage
       and achieve all their goals?
6. Review relationships between security and IT teams
   a. Is there ongoing contention between the groups because of lack of
       coordination/communication?
   b. How can we better improve supporting both groups in combination?
   c. Do our IT and security projects align regularly?

This second list is what IT groups can do to help foster relationships between
cybersecurity teams. As in the case with all these recommendations, this is
not an all-inclusive list, but a good start to open discussion and gain more
insight. This is a starting point for IT operations, development, or engineering groups to consider when engaging with either the SOC, security asses-
sor/auditor teams, or security engineering teams.

1. During what activities do you most often communicate with the secu-
    rity team?
   a. Is it during an incident? Or only when there is suspicious activity
       on the network?
   b. Have you only interacted with the security team with emails?
2. Do you know who the various security groups are within the
    organization?
   a. Do you have an SOC? Have you met the team over meetings or
       only seen emails from them?
   b. Do you have a security engineering team? A threat intelligence
       team?
3. Have you had bad interactions with security in the past?
   a. Have they negatively impacted project timelines or budgets?
   b. Have security controls requested by the security team potentially
       negatively affected the systems or affected uptime?
   c. Have you been given very vague information on vulnerabilities or
       configurations? Has this been a point of frustration for the team?

4. What security frameworks does your team align with?
   a. Is it CIS benchmarks? Is it a Security Technical Implementation Guide (STIG)? How do those settings affect your environment?
   b. Did you have training or an education background in security? Would you like more information from the security team?
5. Are you aware of all the security policies and guidance in the organization?
   a. Is it far too much documentation? Is it not enough? Is it too vague?
   b. Do you want to help shape some of the security guidance based on the technical requirements from customers?
6. Do you include security teams during the onset of projects? Why or why not?
   a. Has this not been done before in the organization? Has it been tried and not been successful?
   b. Would you know who to include on project meetings? Are you unsure of the proper contacts?
   c. Is there no precedent for this? No policies or guidance from the top of the organization?
7. Do you have biases toward security groups based on past experiences?
   a. Are your teams willing to discuss how to move past those negative experiences?
   b. Are you able to meet with the security team casually to discuss what issues have occurred in the past and what would be beneficial for the teams moving forward?
8. Do you feel like security is a moving goal post that can never be achieved?
   a. Has security hindered your projects or operations tasks?
   b. Have you worked hard to implement security settings, only to find that you have more to do after?
9. Do you have a passion or interest in cybersecurity and want to work closer with the teams, but haven't been given the opportunity?
   a. Can you approach management and encourage collaboration between the groups based on this interest?
   b. Is it possible that networking opportunities could be available between IT and cybersecurity groups outside of business hours?

This final list is how cybersecurity teams can first identify gaps and potential issues between either their own groups, or with IT and development teams. Since cybersecurity teams may be small and have many domains covered in one group, or many large groups that are siloed, these questions would need to be tailored to those scenarios. This would be an important area for cybersecurity programs at any maturity level to consider how they interact with other technical and operations groups in the organization (Figure 14.3).

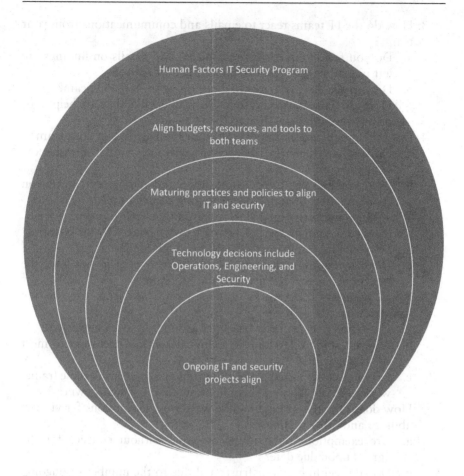

Figure 14.3 Insert diagram IT and cyber collaborate.

1. How have you interacted with IT groups in the past?
   a. Are you brought in during the onset of projects, or at the end of the project to provide a final assessment before it goes to production?
   b. Is it only during security assessments or before audits to remediate findings?
2. Do you know the IT groups within the organization? Operations? Engineering?
   a. Do you communicate with them via email, or have you been on meetings with them?
   b. Have you only interacted with them during times of high stress? Like at the end of a project when you're on a strict timeline?

3. How do the IT teams react to emails and communications from your teams?
   a. Do you feel like security assessments and emails on findings are left unread or without a response from IT teams?
   b. Do you get short or frustrated responses from the IT team?
   c. How are those emails crafted? Do you feel like they are helpful or provide good information to the IT teams?
4. Does the organization support the security objectives of your team?
   a. Do you have the proper budget and resources available to support your projects?
   b. Have you had the time for innovation and automation, or are you spending most of your time managing security tools?
5. What kind of security tools do you have in the environment?
   a. Does your team manage them or are they managed by the IT teams?
   b. Do you have too many tools? Not enough tools?
   c. Do you require open-source tools because you do not have the budget to support the needs of the program?
6. What security frameworks and guidance do you use in the organization?
   a. Does the IT team create baselines around these frameworks?
   b. Are you able to develop the technical controls necessary to meet the frameworks?
   c. Do you feel supported in the organization to implement these frameworks appropriately and communicate that to systems owners?
7. How does the organization handle waivers or exemptions for vulnerabilities and other findings?
   a. Are exemptions ongoing all the time without concern for the agreed upon due date?
   b. Do you feel unheard or frustrated due to the number of ongoing waivers and exemptions?
8. Does security management support your findings and remediation efforts?
   a. Do you find yourself constantly arguing or fighting for findings that won't be enforced to remediate?
   b. Do you have to constantly provide supporting evidence for findings?
   c. Are there constant delays from finding vulnerabilities, to communication with system owners, and ultimately remediating or mitigating them?
9. Does the security team have experience in IT operations or understand the goals of the IT team?
   a. If there is someone with a background in IT – can they help educate the other security team members on what day-to-day operations groups experience?
   b. Is the security team totally cut off from the IT team?

Now that executive leadership, as well as IT and cybersecurity practitioners have an initial set of questions for their teams, a maturity model can be provided and tailored to the answers from the previous exercise. Depending on the answers and how large the teams are, this maturity model can be used to frame improvements between teams. Consider how the previous questions brought up possible pain points, frustrating experiences, or even biases between teams. Then take those answers, and whether from the IT or cybersecurity side, start developing a roadmap for improving relationships and the programs around those responses (Figure 14.4).

1. Based on the initial exercise above, identify the current problems between IT and cybersecurity teams
   a. Hire a behavioral analysis or psychologist consultant to investigate identified behaviors or problems between teams
   b. Are the concerns with *people*, *process*, or *technology*, or all three?
2. Evaluate current documentation, guidance, and processes around IT and cybersecurity

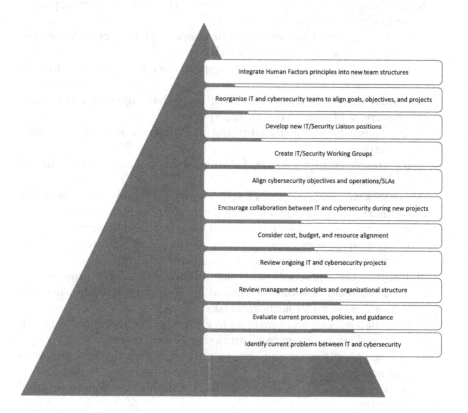

Integrate Human Factors principles into new team structures

Reorganize IT and cybersecurity teams to align goals, objectives, and projects

Develop new IT/Security Liaison positions

Create IT/Security Working Groups

Align cybersecurity objectives and operations/SLAs

Encourage collaboration between IT and cybersecurity during new projects

Consider cost, budget, and resource alignment

Review ongoing IT and cybersecurity projects

Review management principles and organizational structure

Evaluate current processes, policies, and guidance

Identify current problems between IT and cybersecurity

Figure 14.4 Maturity model diagram.

     a. Compare and contrast the documents and identify gaps or conflicting policies that would make projects difficult

     b. Consider how to better enforce security objectives to ensure proper controls are put in place

3. Review current project management practices in the organization
   a. Align IT and cybersecurity projects to meet both groups' missions
   b. Project managers should exist in both IT and cybersecurity teams

4. Review and understand the ongoing IT and cybersecurity projects
   a. IT and development projects should integrate security teams from the onset
   b. Align cybersecurity projects with the IT and enterprise-wide goals

5. Consider how current budget, resources, and personnel influence the IT and cybersecurity teams
   a. Identify possible mismatches between IT and cybersecurity teams in terms of how many personnel they have managing systems
   b. Align IT and cybersecurity budgets based on their goals, current risks, and necessary improvements

6. Encourage IT teams to collaborate with security teams during project development and product creation
   a. Change meeting styles, occurrences, and project management styles to align with this objective
   b. Provide executive leadership support and communications to both teams

7. Encourage cybersecurity teams to align with the operations and management of IT infrastructure and systems
   a. Consider how functionality and operations are affected by security settings
   b. Provide creative solutions for vulnerability findings and remediation efforts

8. Create a working group for IT and cybersecurity teams to meet monthly or quarterly to share blockers, concerns, or possible solutions
   a. Encourage a delegate from each team to attend these meetings
   b. Encourage opportunities for networking and cross-team collaboration outside of high-stress situations

9. Integrate these practices to all new IT and cybersecurity projects
   a. Early identification of technical POC's and individuals who need awareness for projects and tasks
   b. Align policies and processes to encourage collaboration and combined efforts between IT and cybersecurity teams

10. Change team format and structure to align with the new processes and policies
    a. Create new IT or security liaison positions to integrate between teams

b. Create a human factors working group between IT and security teams to continue the understanding of the human element between teams

FINAL THOUGHTS

There are many challenges between IT and cybersecurity groups, and at the center, there are the people who manage these systems. The focus on technology and process are not incorrect, but these should align with the people within the organization. IT teams are stretched thin managing multiple systems and complex environments. Cybersecurity teams typically have smaller budgets and are managing huge environments with very few team members. Both groups have their challenges, and those are only compounded by emerging technology and the increased focus on fast development cycles and a 'rip and replace' culture for tools. But this does not have to be the reality for teams, there is a possibility for these teams to truly enhance each other's projects. Through collaboration, open discussion about their challenges, and management support, these teams can benefit from each other's expertise.

The people that make up our teams come from diverse educational and professional backgrounds, a multitude of technical skill, and incredible passion for the work that they do. Instead of using old ways of developing IT and cybersecurity programs, why not help these teams collaborate better by changing traditional team configurations. Consider developing innovative job descriptions, new types of employees that can help these teams work together and updated organizational structures to align these teams. IT and cybersecurity do not have to be two different conversations or a point of contention between executives. With some empathy and innovation, these teams can really serve the same purpose and align with the business strategy.

If only one thing is taken away from this book, I hope that it is that empathy and understanding are not solely for improving relationships between teams. It is a great place to start, and by improving these relationships, there is a cascading effect to other aspects within an organization. Improvements can be seen in IT projects, lower risk profiles, and ultimately in creating an optimal combination of functionality and security. But this will take time, as does building any sort of trust between teams or changing the way an organization runs. Hire a consultant, be open-minded, and have the courage to dig into these sometimes-complicated problems. It can be difficult to create a culture of self-awareness and willingness to adapt, but with time, care, and encouragement from leadership, all things are possible.

REFERENCE

Siu, K., Moitra, A., Li, M., Durling, M., Herencia-Zapana, H., Interrante, J., Meng, B., & Tinelli, C. (2019). Architectural and behavioral analysis for cyber security. *AIAA 38th Digital Avionics Systems Conference (DASC)*.

Index

Printed in the United States
by Baker & Taylor Publisher Services